From Homeschool to Harvard Without Paying a Cent

Eloisa Minasi

Tested strategies to improve your children's education in TRADITIONAL and HOMESCHOOL settings

Copyright © 2020 Eloisa Minasi

All rights reserved. No part of this book may be reproduced or used in any manner without the prior written permission of the copyright owner, except for the use of brief quotations in a book review.

To request permissions, contact the publisher

Hardcover: ISBN 9781735906614
Paperback: ISBN 9781735906607
Ebook: ISBN 9781735906621

Library of Congress Number: 2020919336

First paperback edition January 2020.

Edited by Dionysia V. Moustakas

Hayesville Barn Press

3881 Downings Creek Road

Hayesville, NC 28904

Published in Fort Lauderdale, Florida

HayesvilleBarnPress@gmail.com

Author's website: www.FromHomeschooltoHarvard.com

"This book addresses the advantages for homeschooling and emphasizes the importance of customizing the curriculum for each student. I believe that intelligence can be enhanced and the author describes strategies to accomplish that. Personalizing is a current concept used in many disciplines and it can be adapted according to each student's individual needs. I recommend the strategies used by the author, especially in this pandemic era when each and every one of us will experience how to perform their functions and tasks remotely and this book can be a good resource to assist parents with their children's remote learning."

Márcia Stephan

Psychologist (*Member of the Pandemic humanity team and also provides emotional health support for cancer patients*)

"I'm in love with this book! As a homeschooling mom myself, I could immediately relate to it once I started reading it. It brought me so much comfort knowing that I'm not the only parent who's faced some of the homeschooling challenges. I definitely feel encouraged and inspired. This book provides great insight for both parents and their children. It is extremely easy to read and very detailed. It can be used as a tool for parents who may be thinking of starting the homeschooling journey, or as a guide for those who have already started it. Overall, I highly recommend it! "

Priscila Davis

Homeschooled her three children (Kindergarten to ninth grade)

"YES, parents are the best teachers for their children! This book is a great tool to help parents that are thinking about or already took over the responsibility of their children's education.

Homeschool is like gardening, we need to cultivate the soil in order to have healthy sprouts growing. The author does an excellent job of sharing her strategies on how her family successfully cultivated their soil and fostered a true lifelong friendship with her children through homeschooling."

Aneliz Butterfield

Homeschool mother of two children (4 and 9 years old)

"The author has a special awareness and sensitivity as to how children learn. Based on her sons' learning styles and needs she was able to guide them to their fullest potential. A very thorough guide."

Rita Chamberlin

Florida Certified Teacher and Homeschool Evaluator

"I was impressed with the author's dedication and ability to supplement her children's education while they were in school. I admire her persistence and perseverance because in addition to being a successful professional in the engineering field, she proved to be an excellent educator! This guide, with such palpable results, should be read by every parent!"

L. Morais

Retired Public School Teacher

ABOUT THIS BOOK

From Homeschool to Harvard Without Paying a Cent shows tried and tested strategies I used over a 10-year period, starting when I supplemented my sons' education during their elementary school years at a public school through a complete transition to homeschooling.

This guidebook fills the gap in the "How to Homeschool" book market. That's because the strategies don't just address the top concerns faced by homeschoolers, they apply to traditional school students as well. The book also benefits parents who were forced to homeschool their children due to the 2020 pandemic.

The fact is every parent should supplement their children's education. If full-time homeschooling is not an option, part-time homeschooling could be the solution to helping your children thrive.

This book provides a wealth of information for new homeschool parents on starting their journey, transitioning from a brick-and-mortar school, supplementing students from traditional schools, choosing curriculums, finding outside resources, developing learning techniques, learning on the road, and integrating extracurricular activities into the school day that help build credentials to improve the chances of getting accepted into a top-tier university.

I also give detailed information about my sons' academic years from elementary, middle, high school, and their transition into college, where my elder son graduated with a neuroscience degree at age 18 and my younger son with an engineering degree at age 19 (both summa cum laude).

As an electrical engineer I was trained to solve problems, so I treated the education system's limitations as an issue I had to tackle and found techniques to overcome the major flaws that exist in today's school system.

CONTENTS

Foreword	1
Preface	3
Acknowledgments	7
Introduction and user guide	9
Chapter One - Helping Children Excel in a Traditional School	**13**
Supplementing: part-time homeschooler	14
Making time to help children	15
How to intervene when a child is placed in a lower-level class	15
Lesson plans designed to fit each child's individual interests	16
Volunteering at your children's school	17
Transitioning from a brick-and-mortar school to homeschool	18
Instill a hunger for learning	19
Chapter Two - Tools to Assist Your Children	**20**
Spiral vs. Mastery approach	20
Learning techniques	23
Speech	25
Mnemonics	26
Foreign language	28
Reward system	29
1. Praising children	30
2. Discipline linked to reward	30
Chapter Three - Non-Academic Skills Play a Role in Academic Success	**33**
Critical-thinking skills	33
Socialization	34
Manners	35
Public speaking	35
Skills to lessen a parent's stress	37
Additional studying techniques	42

Chapter Four - Reasons for Homeschooling — 44
    Comparing homeschooling with brick-and-mortar schools — 44
    Homeschooling during a pandemic — 48

Chapter Five - Homeschool Requirements — 50
    Homeschool law — 50
    Strictest states to homeschool — 53
    Homeschooling space — 55
    Financial expenditure — 56
    Family support — 56

Chapter Six - Homeschool Regimen — 58
    How many hours of homeschooling are needed? — 59
    Learning on the road — 60

Chapter Seven - Should Students be Tested? — 68
    What is the difference between testing and assessment? — 69
    Standardized tests (kindergarten to high school) — 71
    Test-taking benefits — 74
    Optional tests — 75

Chapter Eight - Choosing Curriculum to Foster Independence — 77
    Guaranteeing no educational gaps — 78
    Teaching different age groups — 84

Chapter Nine - Our Curriculum Choices for Mathematics — 87
    Is math an inherited ability? — 90
    How to turn every child into a math person — 91
    Dealing with children who struggle with math — 94

Chapter Ten - Our Curriculum Choices for Writing — 96
    Writing a novel — 105
    Cursive writing — 106

Chapter Eleven - Our Curriculum Choices for Language Arts — 108
    Learning how to read — 108
    Reading with children — 109
    English — 111

Speed-reading	111
Why is reading comprehension important?	112

Chapter Twelve - Our Curriculum Choices for Science — 115

Chapter Thirteeen - Our Curriculum Choices for Social Studies — 122

Geography	126
Civics	129
Additional subjects	131
Physical Education	131
Music, theater, and art	132
Typing	134
Educational television shows	135

Chapter Fourteen - Electives Linked to Career Choices — 137

Main reasons students drop out of college	137
Correlate high school electives to college major	138
Shadowing and volunteering opportunities	139
Middle and high school electives	141

Chapter Fifteen - Outside Resources to Help Alleviate Stress — 144

Second-guessing your ability to homeschool	144
Umbrella schools	147
Co-ops	148
Private schools in collaboration with homeschoolers	149
Enrichment homeschool classes	149
Support groups	150

Chapter Sixteen - Preparing for College — 151

Career goal	151
Traditional versus accredited homeschooler	151
Solutions to ensure a successful transition	152
High school diploma or GED	153
Do all universities require an accredited high school diploma?	154
Preparing a homeschool transcript	156
Earning college credits while in high school	158

    SAT subject tests   163
    Standardized tests for graduate students   163

Chapter Seventeen - Social Behavior   165
    Social skills   172
    No more whining   175
    Put an end to sibling fighting   175
    Should you be your children's referee?   177

Chapter Eighteen - Building a Positive Relationship   178
    Dealing with anger   179
    Ways to communicate and parenting style   179
    Learn to be independent and responsible   180
    Importance of consistency   183
    Positive and negative feedback   184
    Rules and equality   186

Chapter Nineteen - Honor Societies   187

Chapter Twenty - Developmental Stages   189
    Sensorimotor stage (birth to 24 months)   189
    Pre-operational stage (2 to 7 years of age)   190
    Concrete operational stage (7 to 11 years old)   191
    Formal operational stage (11 years and up)   191
    Interacting with children   193
    How is background noise linked to concentration?   194
    Is your child an introvert or extrovert?   194
    Making excuses for children   195
    Is the student underperforming due to anxiety?   196
    Never give up   197
    Injustice can get in the way of compassion   197

Chapter Twenty-One - Be Prepared for Unforeseen Circumstances   199
    A car accident changed my plans   199

Chapter Twenty-Two - From Homeschool to Harvard   201
    Homeschoolers' experiences at Harvard   201
    Important tips   202

Chapter Twenty-Three - Conclusion	204
Bibliography	207
Appendix A	209
Appendix B	211
Homeschool curriculum survey	211
Homeschool Vocabulary	215
About the Author	219

FOREWORD

When Eloisa Minasi contacted me about editing her manuscript on homeschooling, I said, "absolutely." First, editing manuscripts is the part of my job I enjoy most. Second, I've always been intrigued by the concept of homeschooling, as well as a little skeptical.

From Homeschool to Harvard Without Paying a Cent is jam-packed with everything you need to know to supplement your children's education or homeschool them full time. You'll find curriculum and scheduling ideas; suggestions on how to use travel as a learning tool; recommendations and reviews of the best homeschool materials available; and how to keep your kids connected to the outside world.

By the time I turned the last page, several myths had been dispelled, and a new awareness took their place:

- Parents need to take charge of their children's education.
- Our schools need to do better.
- Supplementing a child's education is essential and not as difficult or time-consuming as you might think.
- Homeschooling is an enriching, effective and real alternative to traditional schooling.

On a personal note, you can't spend six months working closely with someone without discovering her true nature. Eloisa is passionate about the importance of education and is driven to share her homeschooling experience with other parents. She wants them know they have options and that no matter what they might think they are up to the task. I hope you find the trip *From Homeschool to Harvard* ... as inspiring as I did.

Dee Moustakas

PREFACE

In January 2014, my two sons and I were stopped at a red light when a drunk driver hit our car going 60 miles an hour. My children, thankfully, were not hurt, but I was severely injured. Major surgery and years of physical therapy relearning how to walk tested every bit of my inner strength. Being able to walk and live each day without excruciating pain is nothing short of a miracle. I thank God every day for giving me another chance in life!

At the time of the accident, I had just finished homeschooling my older son, and was still homeschooling my younger son, who then had to finish his homeschool year with very little assistance. Since he was taught to be independent and self-driven, he not only managed to finish the year successfully, he also was accepted into an engineering program as a full-time college student at age 15. So, yes, I think my homeschool techniques work!

Since I was pretty much bedridden for two years, my husband suggested I use the time to write about our family's successful homeschool journey. *From Homeschool to Harvard Without Paying a Cent* is the result. Writing the book fulfilled my desire to share our homeschool experience with other parents; plus, it took my mind off my chronic pain and my inability to see or walk. (Believe it or not, I discovered you don't necessarily need to see to type!) By February 2016, I had made a full recovery.

This book covers a 10-year period starting when I supplemented our sons' education from their elementary school years at a public school through a complete transition to homeschooling and then college. The techniques and resources shared give parents the tools necessary to provide a solid education, free of gaps that could prove to be challenging if children have to reenter the school system, due to unforeseen circumstances, like my younger son did.

Why did I decide to homeschool our sons? Well, it all started when my older son begged to be homeschooled, because he was not satisfied with the school system. He was in elementary school and already knew that something was not quite right. I was working full-time as an engineer at Motorola and decided to take a leave of absence to prepare myself for this new endeavor. That first year I volunteered at the school, taught math and science, and supplemented both sons' education.

Supplementing is one of the best ways to improve on a school's curriculum, allow children to pursue their interests, and expand their knowledge. I believed that my husband and I were accountable for our children's education, not the teachers. So, I decided to assess the academic areas where my sons needed support and developed lessons to assist them. It only took 30 minutes a day, since everything was well thought out ahead of time. If full-time homeschooling is not an option, part-time homeschooling allows parents to nurture their children's strengths and assist with weaknesses.

According to the National Home Education Research Institute, homeschooling, which is legal in all 50 states, now has more than 1.69 million students learning at home, and that number increases every year. Homeschool parents are motivated by a variety of reasons, including religion, school violence, better academic outcome, less exposure to bullying or peer pressure, flexibility, illness, dissatisfaction with the school system, and fear of the next pandemic.

For students interested in pursuing athletic careers and/or hoping to participate in the Olympics, homeschooling may be the best or only option. A few famous athletes who were homeschooled are Tim Tebow, Serena Williams and Simone Biles.

Regardless of the reasons parents choose to homeschool their children full- or part-time, the end result is always the same: improvement in the outcome of their children's education.

Lack of socialization is one of the strongest arguments against homeschooling, but this preconceived notion is a myth. Homeschool groups arrange field trips, park days, co-ops, parties, clubs, and community service to keep children engaged. My sons were boy scouts, had over 200 hours of community service, and participated in sports throughout the year. Homeschoolers can attend classes outside of the home where they can collaborate and swap ideas with their peers. In addition, public schools allow homeschoolers to participate in their extracurricular activities, clubs, and sports. Parents often hire tutors for subjects that are challenging. While homeschooling, our sons had more free time to participate in extracurricular activities and spend time with friends than when they were in a traditional school. The only difference is that homeschooled students have more direct parental supervision, which is a benefit.

The primary reasons I chose to homeschool were that I was able to capitalize on each one of my children's strengths and build up their weak areas; we could learn outside the home and not be confined to a classroom; I could create the curriculum and take into account my children's preferred learning styles; we were able to adapt our schedule to my children's changing needs; learn history as we visited historical sites across the country; travel without the constraint of the school calendar and learn about other cultures; accelerate or decelerate the pace as needed; and choose the annual test that compares my children with private school students.

In the school system, teaching to the test forces teachers to shape their instructions around each year's test and not concentrate on the content knowledge of each year's curriculum. Homeschool parents can improve curriculum decisions by evaluating how their children are progressing, using tests as a diagnostic tool to create intervention.

This book was designed for veteran homeschooling parents, newbies with children in a brick-and-mortar school who are weighing the pros and cons of homeschooling, and those who want to be prepared for the next pandemic. Homeschool parents can adapt teaching methods to best fit each child's needs to ensure information can be easily absorbed, processed, and retained. I'm writing this book to encourage parents and students, and to let them know that with hard work and determination they can achieve their dreams.

The secret of a child's academic success is parental involvement. It ensures that exploration, critical thinking, mastery of subjects and concepts, and creativity are not abandoned simply because it's more expedient for teachers and the school system.

ACKNOWLEDGMENTS

I am so grateful that I live in a country where we can choose how to educate our children. I would like to thank my two wonderful sons for giving me real- life examples that I could use throughout this book. Without their accomplishments and hard work this book would not be possible.

I could not have completed this endeavor without my amazing husband who supported me throughout these ten years of homeschooling. When I was no longer able to homeschool, due to a car accident, he encouraged me to write this book. The thought of helping parents gave me the strength I needed to recover.

I also would like to express my gratitude to my editor, Dee V. Moustakas from Kodiak Communications, for her ongoing support and encouragement and for amazing insights and guidance towards completion of this project.

I would like to thank my friends and family for their enthusiastic support all these years.

And last, but not least, I am blessed to have met people who are big homeschool supporters. Rita Chamberlin has helped many homeschool families. Thank you for all you do for the homeschool community in Florida!

INTRODUCTION AND USER GUIDE

This book shows tried-and-tested strategies used over a 10-year period starting when I supplemented my sons' education during their elementary school years at a public school and continuing through a complete transition to homeschooling.

It provides detailed information about my sons' academic years during elementary, middle, and high school. These strategies are designed to help parents improve their children's education and smooth out tempestuous parenting waters, whether a child is in a traditional school or homeschooled.

This guide also offers valuable tips on how to start your new journey. As most parents who contemplate if they should homeschool, I embarked on this journey uncertain of what the outcome would be. I wish books written by homeschool parents at the time had included examples of what worked and did not work, so I could have used their successful homeschoolers' experience as my starting point. Instead, books available back then were merely guidelines listing curriculum and information easily found on the Internet. This guidebook fills a gap in the "how to homeschool" book market.

Children tend to mirror adults and are a measure of our success and worthiness. Parents are judged by their achievements and triumphs and compared to other parents in the way they educate their children. In addition, we compare our children to other children on how they behave and interact with others. Every parent strives for their children to be successful, well adjusted, loving, respectful, independent, self-motivated, giving, nice, trustworthy, and well-rounded.

Even before homeschooling, I was exceedingly involved in my children's education. As an electrical engineer I was trained to solve problems, so I treated the educational system's limitations as an issue that I had to tackle. Although I had experience designing complicated devices, such as cell phones, pagers, two-way radios, infrastructure systems, and radar systems, solving the educational system's limitations would require additional insight. My solution was to become a substitute teacher and volunteer at my children's elementary school aiding with science, math, and reading.

Throughout the years, I had a chance to analyze how the school system worked and develop a test plan to improve my children's education by removing the major flaws I encountered. Homeschooling was the way to implement my ideas to ensure my children received the best education. I spent years taking education classes to prepare myself for this new endeavor. Education and children's development classes, along with working in the school system, enabled me to develop innovative ideas. In addition, I am now a certified language teacher (ACCREDITAT-London).

My elder son was homeschooled from middle school, and my younger son from third to eighth grade; in seventh and eighth grade, they both were taking high school classes. Those were our best years together; they had time to be children, to play outside and not be stuck at home doing homework, after a long day at school. Our family had the opportunity to travel all over the United States, Canada, and Brazil –– learning as we travelled, without the constraint of the school calendar.

They flourished and were thrilled to be homeschooled, because it was no longer tedious or repetitious. Since they completed assignments in less time, compared to students in the school system, we had more free time and were able to get ahead in all subjects.

I will share my sons' accomplishments by age 19 to prove that my strategies work. Our results reflect their academic abilities in conjunction with our educational choices. By age 15, both of my sons were attending college on full scholarship (including books and fees) for Engineering and Neuroscience respectively; were selected to participate in the Duke University Talent Identification Program; played on the high school varsity soccer and track and field teams; and were members of the National Honor Society.

My elder son was accepted into Yale University's summer medical and dental education program; won first place at Florida Atlantic University English

Department's best essay writing contest "Human and Nonhuman," at age 15; was offered a position with Florida Atlantic University's Biology Department to work as a lifeline leader teaching three biology discussion classes; wrote a science fiction novel titled "The Fifth Rock"; was an AMSA member; and worked as a "note taker" for the Office for Students with Disabilities at FAU. He also worked on an undergraduate research project that may help combat Huntington's disease by investigating underlying mechanisms of the illness. He graduated summa cum laude from Florida Atlantic University with a bachelor's degree in neuroscience and behavior at age 18.

At age 19, he was accepted into Harvard's Research Scholar Initiative where he is working on neuroscience research at the medical school and taking graduate coursework in preparation for his doctoral program. A stipend, free graduate level classes, and free health insurance, made moving to Boston an easy decision.

My younger son earned a bachelor's degree in electrical engineering (summa cum laude) from Florida Atlantic University. He taught college algebra and pre-calculus at the university's math lab for four years. His passion for engineering was reinforced during an internship at Luminar Inc., which makes Lidar systems for self-driving cars. As a research assistant at the university's research lab, he worked on designing a subsystem for a tethered underwater vehicle that uses artificial intelligence to capture lionfish (invasive species). In addition, he developed an EEG headset integrated with machine learning to retrieve electrical signals from a user's scalp to process and analyze brain waves. One application for this device is to improve prosthetics by allowing paraplegics to control wheelchairs. His project Satori Helmet (EEG headset) won Top Project Award. Today, at 19, he is getting ready to apply for an engineering Ph.D. program. While he is studying for the GRE, he is working for a start-up company designing electronic devices for the United States military.

In addition, they both are CPR/AED-certified, members of the Order of the Arrow, which is the national honor society of the Boy Scouts of America (BSA), and have volunteered hundreds of hours for nonprofit organizations.

They earned their Eagle Scout rank when they were 15 and 17 years old respectively. This is the highest rank achievable in the Scouts program. Only five percent of all boys (and now girls) who join the BSA become Eagle Scouts, mainly because it is arduous and requires determination and discipline. The concentration on leadership and outdoor skills helped them with their Eagle project. Scouts must plan, raise money, and execute projects to benefit nonprofit organizations.

Well-rounded children will have ample opportunities. Universities expect an *unweighted GPA* as close to a 4.0 as possible, a high SAT score, and ranking near the top of the class; in addition, they also seek students who are personable, participate in extracurricular activities, and volunteer work.

Strategies included in this book will benefit all students, whether they are enrolled in a traditional school, homeschooled, or getting ready for the next pandemic.

Homeschooling provides students the opportunity to pursue a career of their choice, since parents will ensure that there will be no "gaps" in their education, especially when it comes to mathematics. I also share the difference between curriculums that apply the spiral versus mastery approach, enabling parents to choose the one that is best suited for each child.

CHAPTER ONE

HELPING CHILDREN EXCEL IN A TRADITIONAL SCHOOL

BOTH OF MY CHILDREN attended a local public elementary school (my younger son up to third grade), were homeschooled for middle school, took most of the High School classes while homeschooling and joined Florida Atlantic University High School program. By the time they were 15 years old, they were full-time college students. We never spent a cent on tuition for school, from elementary school to college! The secret: "Parental involvement" in children's education boosts academic success.

From the time my children were in kindergarten, I was exceedingly involved in their education. I was working full time as an electrical engineer for Motorola when I decided my children took precedence over my career. I took a leave of absence for a year and decided to take education classes, while assisting with math and science at their elementary school.

I acquired tremendous knowledge regarding the school system and its imperfections after becoming a substitute teacher for the Broward County School System. This knowledge gave me the information necessary to develop a plan to improve my children's curriculum and compensate for the school system's flaws, at home, by supplementing academically. My son requested to be homeschooled when he was in second grade; the amount of time he spent at school with little return, frustrated him. He often said, "School is a waste of time. I learn 10 minutes' worth of material, but stay in school for six hours." How amusing to realize that my 7-year-old was disgusted with how little he was learning and that he was wasting his valuable time. Teachers devote countless hours reiterating material, preparing students to perform up to par on standardized tests, and dealing with misbehaving students. Children, who do not require instructional repetition nor have behavior issues, spend most of their time hearing the same material repeatedly.

SUPPLEMENTING: PART-TIME HOMESCHOOLER

Although teachers are the primary educators, parents should have a role in their children's learning process. Why is supplementing children's education so important? It is the only way to nurture curiosity, indulge inquiries that go beyond a school's curriculum, foster creativity, identify their interests, and expand their knowledge.

Homeschool conventions are an efficient way to obtain sound educational tips and are the ideal place to find cutting-edge and popular curriculums at discounted prices. An increased number of schoolchildren's parents are attending these conferences, along with homeschoolers, to improve their children's education.

Politicians often argue about whose job it is to educate children and how to improve the school system. If full-time homeschooling is not a possibility, part-time homeschooling could be the solution to help children thrive. Parents should be accountable for their children's education, even if it's only accomplished on a part-time basis. Involving children in activities that spark their interest is an easy and fun way to supplement and expand on topics that are challenging. Use different strategies to reinforce material learned in school, starting with questions they got wrong on homework and tests. Assess academic areas where children need support and develop lessons based on those topics.

In addition, fun, mental math exercises can be done by younger children at a grocery store, restaurant, or gas station. Ask them to calculate the tip at a restaurant, double the recipe for a cake, or compare prices at grocery stores. Older students can work on projects in engineering, anatomy, programming, or any other topic of interest.

Often, schools are only interested in teaching writing if the state test is scheduled for that year. Once students conclude the test, they ignore that subject and concentrate on the upcoming year's exam. Work with those who show weakness in writing throughout the year to ensure they improve their writing skills.

MAKING TIME TO HELP CHILDREN

Time constraint can be an issue when it comes to part-time homeschooling, because students already attend school six hours a day, followed by hours of homework. Therefore, don't waste their time with assignments that will not benefit them. Use assessment tests to identify areas that need reinforcement.

Identify mistakes made on all homework and tests. After assessing what is necessary to close the gap in their education, the second step is to determine when extra work can be accomplished. My children were not allowed to watch television or play video games during the week; consequently, they had plenty of time for other activities. They played outside and had adequate free time before starting additional assignments. Devote time developing lesson plans before students return from school to ensure time spent on assignments is short and efficient.

A child can accomplish a substantial amount of work in 30 minutes, if everything is well thought out ahead of time. As an example, if a child is learning science at school and the topic is *"pressure and its influence upon fluid behavior,"* build a water gun to show how Bernoulli's equation can be used to calculate pressure of a fluid. I understand that science topics may be intimidating for parents whose expertise is not in that discipline; however, books at the library and the Internet offer a wealth of information on experiments with step-by-step explanations on thousands of topics.

HOW TO INTERVENE WHEN A CHILD IS PLACED IN A LOWER-LEVEL CLASS

Although it is common knowledge that children learn at different paces, the school system insists on labeling children by separating the ones they claim are underachievers by placing them in lower-level classes.

Educators expect to have 25 children progressing at a similar rate. While some schools have accelerated classes, they fail to advance students as their skills improve. As an example, young bilingual children may lag behind in vocabulary (number of words) but catch up in the first few years of elementary school. Language development milestones are the same for all languages; however, even if bilingual students have the same vocabulary as monolingual students, the total number of vocabulary words for each individual language may be reduced when they first start learning a new language. Although this is not a reflection of delayed development, elementary school bilingual students may score lower for English assessment tests that are used to place students in the appropriate English class.

My son, who was learning two languages simultaneously, was placed in a lower- level English class when he was in kindergarten. Since I was extremely involved in the school and interacted with the teacher on a daily basis, I was able to request that his vocabulary skill be retested the following year. He was moved to an advanced English class, because test results showed that he had caught up with more advanced students. Unfortunately, teachers do not reassess student's skills on a regular basis and students get bored because they are under-challenged.

Parents often correlate boredom with children being too smart or gifted, since the work is too easy for them. They should schedule a conference with the teacher to ensure that their child didn't fall through the cracks and is placed in the right level class, before losing focus and interest in learning. Boredom is linked to behavior issues and high dropout rates in high school.

Fortunately, this is not an issue for homeschoolers, because they learn at their own pace at a level defined by the parent. Be prepared, however, to teach high school level material while still in middle school because the one-on-one education allows them to advance rapidly. Let children grow at their own pace, and do not limit them to what the school system thinks they should be learning.

LESSON PLANS DESIGNED TO FIT EACH CHILD'S INDIVIDUAL INTERESTS

Although it is convenient for parents to teach their different-aged children the same subject simultaneously, it is essential to also provide them with alternative activities and curriculum content not yet mastered. Even though my boys are two years apart, we used the same curriculum for science and history. Activities should be of varying complexity and cater to each child's individual needs and personal interests.

Remember, there is no deadline for homeschoolers. Accelerate or decelerate the pace, as needed, and stay on topics of interest to address individual needs. Performance will vary depending on each student's readiness or curiosity. Rest assured, if children are interested in the topic, they will ask questions and maintain sustained concentration.

Since my younger son wanted to be an engineer, I concentrated his studies on designing electronic devices and experiments related to engineering. My elder son's interest was biology, human anatomy, and neuroscience; thus, we studied the human body, including the circulatory system, by means of models and games.

It is imperative to work on subjects that students require assistance with, in addition to areas that they excel in, to ensure that they can build confidence and skill. Part-time homeschool parents have the chance to nurture their children's strengths and provide them with a sense of accomplishment.

VOLUNTEERING AT YOUR CHILDREN'S SCHOOL

Getting to know your children's teachers will help them succeed in school, especially if you volunteer in the classroom. Teachers tend to provide volunteering parents instantaneous feedback on issues that can be addressed immediately. Parents are allowed and even expected to be involved in their children's early school years; however, much less so in middle or high school. By being active in their children's school, parents get familiar with the teacher's routine. Consequently, teachers solicit parents' opinion and share information concerning their children, in an informal way. Parents observe firsthand how their children interact with their peers. If teachers are familiar with each child's skill set, they can best establish how to personalize lesson plans. Parents can help the school by grading papers, photocopying worksheets, assisting in the library, planning field days, or helping in the cafeteria. I assisted in the library and on field days; however, my preference was to support the teacher in the classroom.

I often donated supplies for the classroom and sponsored parties. There are options for working parents who have limited time to be involved. They can help with fund-raising, gather material for projects, or join the Parent Teacher Association (PTA). This organization offers a proven approach where parents can be involved with school policies and functions. The Parent Teacher Organization (PTO) serves the same purpose, but has no affiliation with the PTA and does not always charge dues.

TRANSITIONING FROM A BRICK-AND-MORTAR SCHOOL TO HOMESCHOOL

Homeschool parents can start the transition by providing children with a variety of assessments to determine their abilities and provide them with activities that enhance their education. A free placement test that can determine a child's math level can be found at Saxon Math website. Before spending hours on developing lesson plans, generate a simple test to quantify what areas need concentration. You may have to backtrack and get caught up on basic concepts that were overlooked during their mortar-school years.

My sons were excited about our new endeavor and the transition was not so difficult, because it was child-initiated. I supplemented my children's education and taught them Portuguese for years. Teaching science and other subjects at their school, allowed them to see me as a teacher.

Students are accustomed to having a routine, so make sure to follow a schedule. Routines help students anticipate what they will learn on any given day and when they will have free time or be tested. Make sure to listen to their input and be prepared to make changes to your curriculum. Teaching does not have to happen between 8 a.m. and 3 p.m., although this schedule worked for our family. Students may be part of a swim team or play sports, requiring flexibility in the schedule. Don't try to imitate the public school. Regardless of the reason for removing your children from that environment, don't bring a broken system into your home. Ask your children what they like or dislike about school and replicate things they enjoy. My sons loved recess, so I added that to our schedule, and we would ride our bikes to a local park or play outside on a regular basis.

For those unproductive days when children are sick or other unforeseen situations arise, stay calm and remember it takes four months for homeschoolers to learn what mortar-school students learn in an entire year. In addition, homeschool children test years ahead of their mortar-school peers. Homeschool should be fun, so purchase educational games and take into account each child's learning style.

Parents may feel overwhelmed, and not having "alone time" anymore can be stressful. Look for a physical education program for your children to attend once a week. It is important that they have social interaction with children their own age. If they were part of a varsity sports team or any extracurricular activity organized by a school, they may be able to continue these activities. Most states permit homeschool students to participate in sports at their local school.

INSTILL A HUNGER FOR LEARNING

Parents and educators are responsible for nurturing children's love for learning. Children have a built-in desire to learn, so if they receive educational support during their younger years they will be creative and eager to acquire new information throughout their lives. Using vague terms such as "just do your best" is not a way to offer support. If students earn a low score on a test, they may conclude that they are not smart enough since they tried their best and failed. They may put forth even less effort in the future, since the desired results were not reached.

Successful students are more focused and disciplined. Instill an understanding of good study habits, which will stay with them forever. Review material with students, teach them to summarize concepts and highlight the most important parts of the text. Flashcards are a great revision tool. Writing key terms or questions on one side and definitions or answers on the other side can help kinesthetic learners. For students who need visual cues, drawing a picture on one side of the card is a better study strategy than words.

Everyone can develop a hunger for learning and the better the results, the more knowledge he or she desires to acquire. Children are no different; they learn the importance of knowledge and education through their parents, who are their role models. For parents who did not have the privilege of a college education, being a role model may serve as an incentive for them to achieve that goal.

Support teenagers who may be concerned about breaking with family expectations and attend trade school, instead of college. Trade schools teach skills related to jobs such as welding or plumbing. Unlike college, trade school classes are specific to skills they are interested in. Trade school can be a great option for a reluctant learner who wants to get into the job market faster.

CHAPTER TWO

TOOLS TO ASSIST YOUR CHILDREN

CHILDREN ARE INQUISITIVE BY NATURE, so the best way to promote learning is by answering their questions and expanding on topics of interest. Attuned to learning new information and curious about the world, they are constantly questioning everything. This curiosity can be harnessed to enhance learning.

While some learning techniques emphasize improving children's memory, others improve comprehension. Mnemonics, interactive games, educational TV shows, and educational games are methods that can be applied to supplement children's education.

One effective way to improve your curriculum is to use assessment test results to develop lesson plans. Interleaved learning (spiral) is a great tool to learn geography, civics, art, or music. Is this learning method ideal for math and history or should mastery approach be used? Before I answer this question, let's understand what the differences between these two approaches are.

SPIRAL VS. MASTERY APPROACH

The spiral approach introduces a topic and moves on to a new theme even if students did not master the concept. On the other hand, the mastery approach requires complete understanding of a concept before moving on to a new topic. Understanding the benefits of each approach simplifies the daunting task of selecting a curriculum that benefits your children.

SPIRAL APPROACH: Also known as interleaving, distributing, spacing, or mixing. Interleaving mixes various subjects or topics at the same time, which is contrary to blocked learning, where students learn one topic at a time. The school system and Saxon Math adopted this approach for their math curriculum. The same concepts are covered year after year, with increased depth. This is a great approach for the school system, because if a teacher is assigned a class of 30 students with grades ranging from A to F, repetition is required for those in the lower range of the scale. Unlike homeschool students, teachers cannot require a 90 percent on exams before moving on to new topics. Seventy percent suffices for public school students to pass to higher grades. Students, who earned a "C" in math, could benefit from this method because material will be repeated year after year. However, an "A" student does not need the endless repetition.

Math builds upon previous knowledge, so choosing a method that benefits your children is vital. Since my sons went to public elementary school for a few years, we knew the spiral approach did not work for us. The same material was repeated year after year and, although they added to the complexity of the concept learned, my sons did not like the repetition. So, I decided to switch to a mastery approach.

MASTERY APPROACH: Video Text Interactive uses this method. In a mastery program, students do not move on to a new topic until the current concept is mastered. Unless students reach a predetermined level of mastery (80 to 90 percent), they are not allowed to progress to the following section.

Homeschool parents may choose to assess students after three or four sections and combine different skills when performing assessment tests. Mixed problems enable the brain to retrieve concepts learned in previous sections and can easily be implemented using a mastery curriculum, even though experts claim that this is the benefit of the spiral approach.

I combined this method with regular assessments to determine if my sons

> *We used RightStart Math for K-4th grade, Saxon for 5th -6th, and then Videotext Interactive for Algebra and Geometry. This provided a strong enough math foundation so that both of my high schoolers passed their College Algebra CLEP at age 13 and 15!*
>
> **JO (North Carolina)**

were ready to move on to the subsequent topic. Repetition can be introduced to the mastery approach, but parents have full control over how much redundancy is needed.

It is impossible not to revisit previous material when learning algebra or calculus, since most concepts learned are applied in future lessons. Most curriculums that apply mastery approach put emphasis on individual lessons; however, problems are drawn from previous lessons and presented in an intermixed order after a few sections. The benefit of not mixing problems for every section is that students can learn each skill individually and will be able to solve a much larger sample of problems for each technique. Let's say, for example, that students are learning how to solve a quadratic equation, which can be solved in five different ways. So, the mastery approach would have five lessons, which include factoring, square root method, completing the square, quadratic formula, and graphing.

By learning each technique individually, students have the opportunity to solve a larger sample of problems applying each method before solving problems in an intermixed order. Sometimes there are advantages of using one method over another, and the wrong technique can result in awkwardly wrong answers. The mastery approach presents more examples for solving a quadratic equation using different techniques, while the spiral method may give a smaller percentage of problems. Eventually, both methods allow problems to be juxtaposed and require students to choose the best strategy; in addition, in both cases a review of all lessons is offered before a cumulative exam.

The combination of mastery and spiral methods forces the brain to focus on searching for concepts learned in earlier lessons. The process of figuring out which formulas to apply when solving problems strengthens neural connections.

Determining whether the spiral is better than mastery is subject-specific. The mastery method was the best option for our family when studying math and history. On the other hand, the spiral method had its benefits for other subjects.

Our results using the mastery approach for mathematics: My younger son interviewed for a tutoring position at Florida Atlantic University's math lab at age 15. As part of his interview, he had to solve a calculus problem on a blackboard and explain each step in front of three university professors. He got the job on the spot and has tutored at the university for almost five years.

Which method should you use for other subjects?

English, geography, art, music, and civics are examples of subjects that may benefit from the spiral approach. While math uses a process of logic, other subjects are composed of isolated facts. The spiral method along with mnemonics, rhymes, songs, and acronyms can help with these subjects.

It would be impossible to learn how to play guitar or piano without repetition. Most research compares both approaches and concentrates on these areas of study. Using the interleaving method to learn music and alternating between chords and scales have shown to produce better recall of the skill. The same can be said for studying art and getting students to recognize paintings by different artists.

Since students differ in levels of preceding knowledge, methods used to supplement their education are individualized. Regardless of what method is chosen, use it in conjunction with lesson plans that take your child's preferred learning style into consideration.

The Program for International Student Assessment (PISA), which tests high school students around the world, has found that the top seven scoring countries adopted the mastery approach for mathematics. (Most of the school systems in the United States use the spiral approach.) PISA's results place the United States in 38th place, out of 71 countries.

LEARNING TECHNIQUES

VAK learning style uses visual, auditory, and kinesthetic learning strategies. Although there are several learning style models, this is one of the most popular. These three modalities can be used to learn new information, although we all have a preference that makes learning more effortless.

In general, schools rely heavily on books and repetition, while homeschoolers can learn on the go and take advantage of kinesthetic, auditory, and visual learning. Although in a school setting it is impossible to cater to each student's preferred learning style, conventional schools recognize the importance of individualized learning and are increasingly shifting in the direction of a more hands-on methodology.

Homeschool parents can adapt teaching methods to best fit each child's needs to ensure information can be easily absorbed, processed, and retained.

At the school setting, elementary school students are presented with information using the kinesthetic style, moving to visual presentation for middle school, and auditory style for higher grades. Rarely do teachers present information using all three learning styles.

Although many high-ranked universities (Caltech, UC Berkeley, Yale, Harvard, and UCLA) are advocates for VAK methodology, you also will find opponents. Children will learn regardless of what learning style you apply; however, a well thought-out curriculum helps them retain information. Using the three modalities, but emphasizing each of my children's preferred style, provided us with excellent results.

"Customizing teaching" to account for each student's differences and preferences is a daunting task in the schools; however, easily accomplished in a homeschool environment. Since I will be using these terms throughout the book, let's review the three styles here:

1. Visual learners prefer to observe objects, including diagrams, pictures, charts, etc. They like to summarize what they learn; and they absorb information best through demonstrations, charts, videos, or any visual material.

2. Kinesthetic learners choose hands-on experiences and like to scan the material before reading. They use color highlighters to take notes. They have a preference for movement, so concentration is lost when external stimulation is absent.

3. Auditory learners like to listen to information, so dialogue is important. Talking to a colleague or listening to a lecture or recording is their best way to learn.

My younger son's dominant learning style was visual. Since the elementary schoolteachers were unable to cater to his preferred learning method, I supplemented with activities to reinforce concepts learned in school. As a visual learner, he learned best by seeing graphic displays, illustrations, and videos. My elder son's dominant learning style was auditory. Since an auditory learner can also benefit from multimedia applications, I could incorporate my younger child's lesson plans into his.

SPEECH

Students with speech delay are identified by teachers at the public schools and evaluated by a speech therapist. Speech therapy is free, and sessions are held during school hours.

What if the student is homeschooled and does not have access to the public school's speech therapist? Although the best option is to consult with a professional speech therapist, free articulation screen tests are readily available online. These tests can help parents assess if a child's speech is typical for his or her age or delayed. A picture related to a word and its sound position (initial, middle, or final) is shown to help identify if the target sound is correct.

Developmentally appropriate sounds in words by age:

1. Age two: P, B, M, H, and N sounds.
2. Age three: D, T, K, G, and W sounds.
3. Age four: NG, F, Y, CH, J, L, SH, S and V sounds.
4. Age six: S, L, B blends.
5. Age seven: TH sound.

My younger son had speech therapy at the elementary school for three years with little improvement. Since consistent practice and repetition is necessary to overcome an articulation disorder, 30 minutes of therapy twice a week was not sufficient. In addition, the therapist treated several students during the 30-minute session, and they all had different speech problems. I requested instructions on how to work with my son at home, and the therapist was thrilled to provide articulation worksheets and oral exercises. I summarized everything into a spreadsheet, including exercises that I wanted my son to do for five minutes in the morning and afternoon. Although the therapist was helpful, I obtained most of the information from the Internet.

Below are examples of exercises, which show that speech therapy can also be done in a fun and interactive manner.

1. Put peanut butter on the child's lip and ask him to lick all around the upper and lower lips. Tongue exercise elicits perfect speech.

2. Take a frozen banana and put it on a Popsicle stick. Add chocolate syrup and graham cracker crumbs on top of it. Ask the child to lick the graham cracker crumbs off the banana. This activity provides tactile stimulation to the child's mouth. After doing all the exercises needed, the child gets to eat the treat.
3. Place two marshmallows on an apple wedge with peanut butter. Have the child try to take a marshmallow off with her lips.

Strengthening speech muscles improves communication. If paying for a speech pathologist is an issue, consult with a professional to determine the problem area. Once diagnosed, the therapist can provide a list of exercises needed to improve your child's speech delay.

MNEMONICS

Mnemonics are simple strategies that can be used to aid information retention. Although students need to understand math or grammar rules, memorization can assist in learning facts for other subjects. I still remember songs I learned in fourth grade, emphasizing historical facts that were incorporated into the lyrics. Songs related to a historical date or historical figure allow students to recall names, places, and dates.

Mnemonics uses the right side of the brain, where rhymed patterns and images translate information into a form that students will remember. Eventually, this information is consolidated into long-term memory. Acronyms can be formed using the first letter of each word to remember formulas, musical notes, or any fact students are required to remember. Mnemonics is also used for foreign-language acquisition and medical treatment for patients with memory deficit.

Sayings and rhymes can help students remember grammar, spelling, math, or even historical facts. Everyone knows the princi<u>pal</u> is your <u>pal</u>. Also, the ABC song helps children remember the alphabet.

Multiplication can be learned using a unique method created by Multiplication.com –– a funny picture linked to a story helps kids memorize multiplication facts.

> *"Many years ago, there was a giant who lived in a forest. People were afraid of him because he was so big. The lonely giant decided to go to the city to find some friends. During his journey to the city, he saw some construction workers putting up a new sign. The giant walked up to one of the workers*

and tapped him on the shoulder. When the man saw the giant, he dropped the sign. The SIGN (9) landed on the giant's SHOE (2) and his toe started ACHING (18)".

Multiplication.com

The knuckle mnemonic helps students recall which months have 30 or 31 days. Knuckles have 31 days, spaces have 30 days, and February has 28 or 29 days!

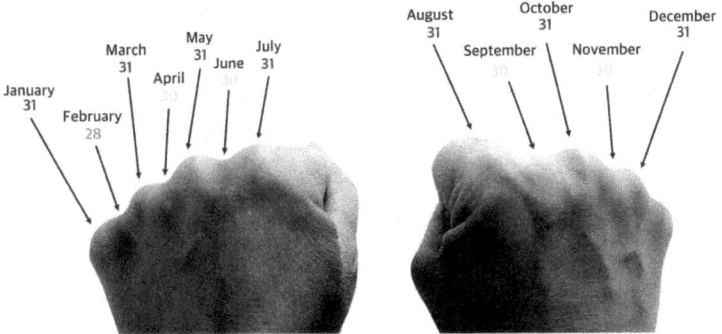

My husband still remembers the following: 30 days have September, April, June, and November. All the rest have 31, except for February. (Using your knuckles is easier!)

FOREIGN LANGUAGE

The study of foreign language is part of the curriculum in most countries, starting in elementary school. Although Americans live a productive life without knowing another language, today a second language is a requirement to enter college and beneficial in getting a higher paying job.

Proficiency in a second language enhances opportunities in this global economy, since numerous companies do business abroad.

Thomas H. Bak, Ph.D., a lecturer at Edinburgh's School of Psychology, performed a study on learning a second language. He claims that it improves brain function, no matter when it is learned. Researchers found that students who spoke a second language had enhanced concentration compared to those who spoke only one.

Learning a foreign language can benefit children in the long run. A Latin-based language opens the door for children to learn other Latin-based languages. I speak Portuguese, which is a Latin-based language; consequently, it was effortless to learn Spanish due to the similarities between the languages. Germanic languages are not quite the same, since people who speak English will not learn German or other Germanic languages effortlessly.

Learning a second language is easier when children are young. The Spanish alphabet is similar to the English alphabet, making this language easier to learn. Considering the number of Spanish-speaking immigrants living in the United States, having the ability to speak Spanish can be an asset when entering the workforce.

Often, homeschool parents teach their children the language they grew up speaking, due to family ties. Although teaching my children to speak my native language was not a simple undertaking, we succeeded. We used Rosetta Stone in addition to books purchased in Brazil. Rosetta Stone teaches foreign language without translation, allowing students to hear a specific word and see a picture associated with it. In our case, the voice recognition program was not always precise, because the software did not understand a native speaker. (This software bug may have been corrected by now.) Combine this software with movies and games, and allow children to interact with native speakers to practice what they learn.

No matter what the motivation for learning a foreign language, it will certainly be beneficial to everyone.

Using mnemonics to learn a foreign language

Certain sounds are unique to specific foreign languages, so replicating these sounds can be challenging. Some examples are the "th" sound, which is unique to English, and the Spanish "rolling r."

When I was learning English, I came up with ways to correlate difficult words with visual cues or sounds used in my native language. I will use examples in Spanish, since it is a language that the mainstream can identify with. For example, the English word bread is pan in Spanish. To remember this word in Spanish, visualize cooking the *bread* in a *pan* and associate the target word with a visual picture.

If a word is paired with a visual equivalent, it is easier to recall. Eventually, you will remember the word in Spanish and not necessarily remember how it was correlated with the visual cue. If the word is too long, break it into easy-to-remember syllables. The mind has an extraordinary ability to store images, especially non-typical ones.

To learn how to pronounce the word, I would write the word the way it sounded in Portuguese. For example, the word *technical* sounds similar to "te" "qui" "ni" "cou" in Portuguese. The same technique can be used for other languages.

Another fun activity is to use onomatopoeia to learn a new language, vocabulary, and geography. Onomatopoeia is a word that mimics the sounds animals, humans, or objects make. Animal sounds are different around the world. I recall going to a wedding in Italy one year and found myself having dinner with guests from Germany, Italy, Brazil, and Spain. My husband could only speak English, so I came up with the idea of comparing a rooster's crowing sound for each country. It was quite entertaining, and we were able to talk and laugh without understanding each other's language. This phenomenon is not limited to roosters. This is a fun way to incorporate geography when learning a foreign language.

REWARD SYSTEM

Celebrate every milestone. Treat children to a special lunch or outing after every big accomplishment. Local businesses offer freebies after seeing a student's report card with A's and B's. Report card rewards vary from state to state and not all businesses participate. To avoid frustration and disappointment, call each business to ensure they still offer these programs.

Below is a list of businesses that participate in this amazing program:

- Applebee's: The A for apple rewards children with a free kid's meal. This program is through the school only.
- Baskin-Robbins: Offers a free scoop of ice cream.
- Chick-fil-A: A student with an A or B report card can earn an eight-piece chicken nugget meal or free ice cream. Perfect attendance is also awarded. The school needs to contact them.
- Chuck E. Cheese: Students earn game tokens.
- Cold Stone Creamery: Free ice cream with straight-A report card. Kindergarten through fifth grade students can participate.
- McDonald's: A straight-A report card earns a free happy meal.
- Pizza Hut: Three A's on the report card get a free personal pan pizza and a small soda or milk.
- Wendy's: Students get a treat if they show a report card with A's and B's.

Praising children for small accomplishments

Offering children positive reinforcement helps them understand that they are in charge of their own success and it motivates them to do better. Praise them for their curiosity, effort, and persistence. These qualities result in success not only in school, but also in life.

Try not to share children's grades with other parents or students because comparing children's performances sets an unrealistic measure of success, taking away what really matters –– "personal improvement."

Discipline linked to reward

Discipline is necessary to ensure children learn their boundaries. As children interact with each other or adults, it becomes evident which ones are disciplined by their parents. Disciplining children does not mean physical punishment or verbal abuse. It encompasses a set of rules and behaviors that help them navigate future relationships and deal with challenges they will face in life. Respecting others and recognizing appropriate behavior are some examples.

For children to learn how to manage their feelings and control their behavior, also known as self-monitoring, takes time and patience. Do not expect a

2-year-old to learn these skills. Discipline needs to match your children's ability to understand what is asked of them, based on their developmental level.

As they mature, children can successfully deal with challenges and temptations. Positive discipline is calmly communicated and children are made aware of what is an acceptable behavior. Praising children for their efforts sends the message that they are making the right choices.

Below are techniques I used with my children, with positive results.

- Star system for young children: A calendar was given to each of my sons, and every time I "caught" them making the right choice, I added a star to the calendar for that day. Whether children are helping siblings with homework or working on chores without being asked, they are making the right choice. Make sure to explain why they are earning a star. Although stars were awarded for noble behavior, they also were removed for unacceptable conduct. Fights with siblings, talking back, or any inappropriate behavior would be grounds for removing a star. By the weekend, stars could be exchanged for privileges. A chart system listing fun activities was created and placed next to the calendar. Each activity had a number of stars associated with it, meaning that my children could trade their stars for each one of these fun activities. For example, they were allowed to play video games for two hours on the weekend. However, they could buy more time with "star points." One extra hour of video games took 10 stars; watching TV beyond the time allotted cost 10 stars; and staying up late five stars. Allow children to suggest adding or removing items from the list and make sure the list reflects each child's interest. Immediate gratification reinforces positive behavior; but never bribe children by offering rewards for good behavior.

- Often, children have a difficult time with certain behavior expectations and may need time to learn and adjust. Jot down three behaviors that need improvement. Every time they behave that way, put an "x" next to it and allow them to make the same mistake three times before stars are removed. After the second week, remove a star each time they misbehave. Once children master all three skills, add three additional items.

Children can detect when we are insincere, so make sure you mean what you say. Find a resolution to problems together, allowing children to offer ideas. Make sure to put emphasis on effort, as well as results.

CHAPTER THREE

NON-ACADEMIC SKILLS PLAY A ROLE IN ACADEMIC SUCCESS

NON-ACADEMIC FACTORS, SUCH AS MOTIVATION, emotional control, and attitude play a big role in academic success. Students with these traits are more likely to have a higher GPA in college. Time management, good study habits, and critical-thinking skills should also be addressed during student's school years. Below are tips on skills to help children thrive.

CRITICAL-THINKING SKILLS

Such skills ought to be emphasized in any sound educational program. Often, controversial topics such as greenhouse gases and depletion of the ozone layer are covered in the news and newspapers. Parents should challenge children to ask probing questions in response to these and other popular claims, because these are frequently topics for high school and college essays. Students should be encouraged to verify scientific claims and question faulty assumptions.

Critical-thinking skills are essential to improving testing scores and assisting with learning math, reading, science, social studies, and writing. Children can often read at a young age, yet critical-thinking skills required for comprehension develop over time. Reading comprehension can be viewed as an in-depth analysis of a child's analytical skill.

In order to outperform in math, students need deductive and inferential reasoning to be able to solve word problems. In-depth analytical skills equate to higher test scores.

SOCIALIZATION

One of the biggest misconceptions of homeschooling is that students do not socialize with other children. A paradigm that has become a myth!

When my sons were in brick-and-mortar school, they barely had time to play outside or meet with friends due to the amount of daily homework. In addition, they both played soccer at a local park and from time to time could not even go to practice. Homeschooling for middle school turned out to be a blessing. They could be kids again and participate on field trips, meet with friends any time during the week, and play sports. On Thursdays, my sons spent the whole day with a large group of homeschoolers playing sports at a local park.

How much time do school children spend socializing with peers? How does that compare with homeschoolers?

Let's analyze how school's socialization time stacks up against homeschoolers' social interaction with their peers. Most teachers frown upon children socializing during instructional hours, so unless students are working on a project together there is no socialization. Although the group settings at schools create an opportunity for students to socialize, I found that my children's interaction with other students proved to be limited due to its structured setting. Physical Education was scheduled for 40 minutes (twice a week) and daily recess for 30 minutes, adding up to three hours and 50 minutes of interaction with other children a week. While they had some opportunity to socialize during lunch, most of the time they were called to attention for talking at lunch and didn't always have a choice to sit with their friends. Of course, this varies depending on the school and teachers.

How did that compare with my sons' experience with homeschool? They interacted with friends for nine hours on Thursdays, compared to less than four hours in a school setting. They were free after 3 p.m. which left them to get together with friends, play sports, learn how to play guitar, read their favorite books, and bike every afternoon. How wonderful to see my sons enjoy their childhood, have time to participate in Boy Scouts, and attend campouts once a month.

Home-educated children tend to spend time out in the real world, interacting with people of all ages. Except for Montessori schools, children in a traditional school setting are grouped with same-age children. Granted, this is the most efficient way to educate children in the school environment, but it doesn't provide the exposure to older children and adults that homeschoolers get. Similar to school children, homeschoolers volunteer in their communities, join church groups, scouts, dance, and other activities. Homeschoolers have more time for extracurricular activities, which provides opportunities for new friendships and learning experiences.

The public school was a perfect environment for my sons to learn to follow school rules, learn to take instructions from other adults, and receive behavioral guidelines; however, peer-to-peer socialization encompassed a small percentage of their day.

Although I believe that school can be a good source of positive social situations, it is also a source for negative interactions. Bullies, drugs, exposure to bad behavior are some examples.

MANNERS

Children are not born with the ability to know right from wrong, how to interact with people, or behave in social gatherings. Parents need to be their children's role models and teach them to say thank you, please, excuse me, and sorry.

Good manners convey a sense of gratitude, rather than entitlement. It helps a candidate who is interviewing for college or a job to stand out from other applicants. Well-mannered and well-behaved youngsters impress everyone.

Parents fail to realize that children are not born with certain skills. Children need to be taught how to answer the phone, make eye contact, shake hands (maybe not during a pandemic), and offer assistance to someone in need. Encourage children to place phone calls, accept package deliveries, and order their own meals at a restaurant. These everyday tasks refine social skills.

PUBLIC SPEAKING

Public speaking can be informative, persuasive, and/or entertaining. Every professional can benefit from being an informative public speaker. A doctor may lecture to medical students, teachers must lecture to students and present information to parents and firefighters may need to give a demonstration on fire safety. An elected official should be an expert on persuasive speaking to ensure continued career success. The ability to think critically is essential, and it can be developed with practice.

My children practiced this skill when they applied for positions in their Boy Scout troop. The opportunity to speak in front of a group of teenagers and scout leaders was a valuable lesson. Since the troop had to vote for the boys who applied for positions, the speeches had to be entertaining and persuasive. Pledges were made to make camping experiences more fun or improve weekly meetings.

The communication merit badge requires scouts to interview city officials and communicate with adult leaders via email and in person, without parents' involvement. My sons held leadership positions, where they were in charge of a group of scouts and had to teach younger scouts skills required by the Boy Scout organization. One of the requirements for the citizenship merit badge was to interview local authorities on turtle protection at our local beaches. They also participated in City Council meetings that dealt with irregularities with local building permits.

A public speaking merit badge allows scouts to deliver presentations using visual aids and body language.

Homeschoolers can learn about public speaking using FLVS, interactive curriculum, co-op classes, or the YMCA program.

- Florida Virtual School's public speaking class teaches techniques to reduce anxiety, theory, and practice of speaking in public.
- The *Learn Public Speaking* DVD is a program that presents the topic in a simple way. It focuses on using outlines, confidence-building skills, and strategies to support arguments.
- Co-op/Club: Parents can either create a public speaking club or join a local group. Most co-op groups involve children in persuasive, personal, and demonstration speeches.
- YMCA allows students to participate in Youth Governors Conferences and Judicial Competitions. The Youth in Government program's mission is to help future generations become active citizens.

Children can practice demonstrative speaking after performing a science experiment by presenting results in a clear and concise manner. Informative speakers simply explain a concept, while persuasive speakers have to convince the audience of their viewpoint. Persuasive writing is about how the writer feels, thinks, or believes about a topic. In a way, children already have this mindset. Being persuasive is an innate quality in children. Explaining to parents how playing video games improves their problem-solving skills and helps with eye and hand coordination is an example.

Brainstorm a few topics and have them write about one of the themes. They should present their position to the family or a group of homeschool students.

SKILLS TO LESSEN A PARENT'S STRESS

Time management

Teach students to develop strategies for time management at a young age, since this is a valuable skill that benefits them all through their lives. Many adults struggle with time management, leading to stress.

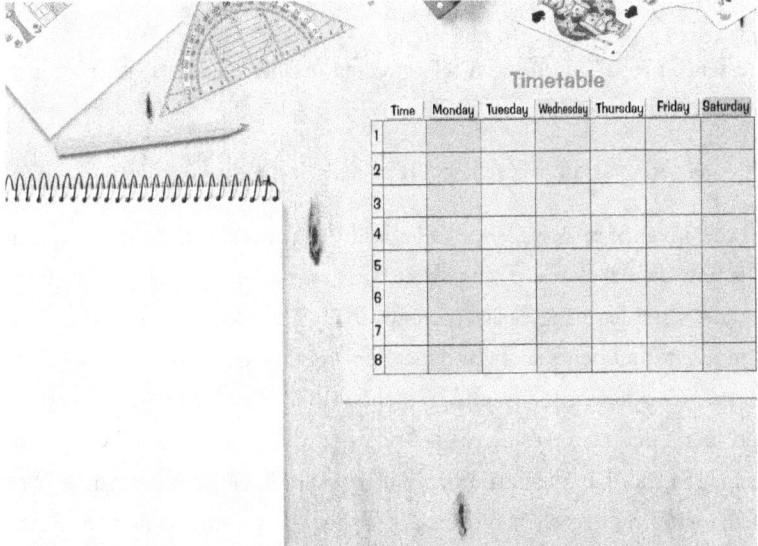

Below are some time management skills that would not only benefit the homeschooler, but also the parent:

- When things get overwhelming, take a break. Go for a walk and relax. Obviously, this would not apply for a child who is taking a standardized test.
- Avoid procrastination. Teach your children to complete tasks and study ahead of time.
- Break tasks into smaller steps. Make sure to assign projects that are complex enough and require some planning on the student's

part. Teach them how to break the project down and set a deadline for each section.

- Prioritize tasks. Make sure students learn this skill by prioritizing important tasks. People tend to start with the easy tasks, not realizing that the more complex assignments will be more time consuming.
- Create a to-do list and update it daily. Most students own a cellphone and/or a computer, so they can use Google Calendar to set reminders of important deadlines.
- Organize your time and identify activities that are unnecessary.

Self-learning skills

It is essential to teach children self-directed learning skills, to think for themselves, and the importance of self-learning.

Use the following strategies to encourage self-learning:

With the advance of new technologies and the growth of the Internet, information is now available at our fingertips. This easy access to a wealth of information makes self-learning easily accomplished. This skill boosts comprehension and motivates students to be independent, giving them the ability to explore any topic of interest. If my children showed interest in a specific topic, they would spend extra time researching and expanding on the idea. When students are engaged in what they are learning, they retain more information. Provide students with the necessary resources that help them process new information.

Allowing children to make their own decisions

Decision making is a skill that children develop with time. Allow them to make choices on things that will not impact their lives, showing that you trust them. Gradually allow them to make critical decisions. Provide unstructured play when they are young and allow them to make choices. In childhood, the priority should be free play. A child who plays in the park with friends will learn to negotiate, interact with other children, empathize, listen to others, evaluate risks, solve problems, develop courage, and be creative. Allow them to choose which toy to play with, which movie to watch, or which game to play. These decision-making processes provide them with the building blocks necessary for independent thinking.

My sons would select and plan our field trips, choose what to wear, pick their friends, or choose what books to read. As they grew, the decisions became more important and the consequences greater.

If you allow a child to decide what to wear, you take a chance he or she might wear a Spiderman outfit to go to the bank, including the mask. I almost intervened one day, but decided that my 4-year-old could walk into a bank wearing a mask and not create chaos. People at the bank were staring and giggling. All the attention made him uncomfortable, and he decided not to repeat the experience the next time we went to the bank. Ironically, I never thought there would be a day that I would go into a bank with a mask on until the coronavirus pandemic!

Allow your children to choose their own friends. One day at a playground, my son was not interacting with this one child and I asked him, "Why don't you play with Joshua? He seems to be a nice kid." He instantaneously replied, "Mom, I could never be friends with him, he always gets in trouble at school and I do not want him to get me in trouble too." Speechless, I just accepted his judgment.

Parents have the obligation to listen to their children and respect their concerns. Try not to diminish their apprehension, even if you do not agree with them. Children learn to make decisions and may not always make the best choice; however, a wrong decision will turn into a learning experience. If children have a close relationship with their parents, they will consult with them on how to proceed when they are confronted with making a difficult decision.

When my children had homework questions, I would ask them to read the question out loud and explain what they thought was being asked, allowing them a few minutes to answer. If they are close to understanding, offer hints and allow them to figure it out for themselves. Although it is easier to just offer an answer that does not allow them to grow more confident. The same is true with life decisions.

Motivation comes from within a person and cannot consistently be triggered by exterior pressure. If children understand the actual reason why parents insist that they apply themselves, it presents them with the incentive to succeed. Babies learn how to speak as their parents interact with them. The motivation to learn is natural and an inherited human behavior; consequently, it is natural for children to imitate people they admire and identify with. However, the best motivation is the motivation within; meaning when people feel satisfaction when they succeed, it motivates and inspires them to improve.

Children should understand the importance of having a good GPA and how it correlates with their test grades. In addition, if they understand how grades will affect them later in life, they will be motivated to study and, in return, increase their opportunities to be accepted into college and succeed in life. When I got a job at Motorola as an Electrical Engineer, I had to share my GPA with the Human Resources Department because they used that number to come up with my initial salary. It's a fact: Professionals with higher GPAs receive better compensation. Personal motivation results in satisfaction when succeeding.

Also, teaching children the correlation between what they learn in school to the real world is crucial; it stimulates their desire to continue to learn. If they are interested in learning a new language or a new skill, provide them with the necessary tools. Showing enthusiasm and encouraging children's interests allows them to grow and explore the world. Celebrate even the smallest achievements. I used to reward my sons for their extra efforts. If they were "caught" in the act of making the right decision, whether it was with extra school work or assisting each other with homework, I would award them a star. Praising children shows them that you notice positive traits and not their faults. Giving them the attention they want increases their desire to continue to do the right thing. (Chapter two covers the star reward system, where children can exchange the stars earned for good behavior for specific activities.)

Children should be able to link their desired possessions, such as cellphone and video games with their parent's lifelong efforts and understand that their hard work allows them to purchase those items.

At Motorola, when employees failed to complete an assignment they would receive a bad yearly review, which would reflect on their annual raise. If they continued to fail, they would be on the list for future layoffs. These are the results of poor choices.

Students who are able to correlate different professions with the subjects they are learning at school are more likely to put in extra effort, because they understand why they must acquire specific knowledge.

If children choose to go out with friends instead of studying for a test and the decision results in a low grade, they just learned that a bad decision has repercussions. Bad consequences are the result of unfortunate choices.

How to handle failure

"Failures are finger posts on the road to achievement." **C. S. Lewis**

People will fail at some point in their lives, yet this experience can be used for self-improvement. While some people see failure as an opportunity to improve themselves, others use excuses and procrastination to avoid failure. The famous excuse "I did my homework, but forgot to bring it" is often used to avoid failure due to a student's lack of ability or responsibility. These students tend to focus on non-academic activities to compensate for academic inability.

It is imperative to build positive relationships with children and change their attitude toward schoolwork. Although parents should work with children on improving studying habits, empower them to take responsibility for small tasks. If my son forgot his homework at home, would I take it to school for him? No, I would not. Being overprotective and not allowing children to falter, denies them the experience to fear failure.

Consider a tutor for subjects that are challenging or if interpersonal tension interferes with the way of teaching. Assist with problem-solving techniques and encourage independent effort. Children may get bored if they are placed in a lower-level class that is too easy for them. For math, determine if they are at the appropriate level by giving them placement tests. Match children's math level according to their skill and readiness. I tested both of my children's math skill using Saxon placement tests and found these online tests pretty accurate. My sons were learning high school level Algebra I math in sixth grade.

Note-taking is a skill that assists students who feel overwhelmed by chapter after chapter of new information. To help with this, highlight boldface words, headings, and captions (text that appears below images) and summarize the content.

In a school setting, it is easier for teachers to teach everyone the same material and not cater to individual students.

ADDITIONAL STUDYING TECHNIQUES

Be Prepared for Class

Reading the material before attending class makes it easier to follow the lecture. Most of the steps below apply to high school or college-level classes, but parents can help a middle school student become familiar with these strategies.

- Review lecture notes for that week. The chapter summary, combined with notes, provides familiarity with new concepts.
- Make a list of questions for the teacher or professor.
- Students spend most of the class taking notes, word for word, on material being taught. Break this cycle and recognize the importance of being prepared for class. It is vital to listen to the lecture, and only jot down key ideas.

Bad Study Habits

Refrain from re-reading your notes to study for a test. This bad study habit assumes that the teacher will be testing the student on memorization skill. Teachers expect students to integrate concepts taught during the year and to understand how a concept is related to other ideas.

Generate a study plan listing what you want to accomplish. If your child spent hours studying and the results were not optimum, come up with a better study plan. Make sure to remove any distractions, such as a cellphone.

Teach What You Learned

After students study for a test, ask them questions or have them teach the material to a sibling. When they are comfortable enough with the material and can convey the information to another person, they undoubtedly have mastered the concepts.

Flashcards

Students can self-test by using flashcards. Virtual flashcards, such as Quizlet, can be an effective way to learn any subject. For math, put the multiplication fact on one side and the answer on the other side. The same can be accomplished for vocabulary, chemistry, geography, and history.

Concept Mapping

This is a graphical representation used to reorganize information and recognize the connection between concepts. It is a visual strategy to learn complex material to analyze, compare, and contrast information.

CHAPTER FOUR

REASONS FOR HOMESCHOOLING

HOMESCHOOLERS CAN INITIATE THEIR JOURNEY at any time of the year, and there has never been a better time to join the homeschool community. Schools all over the world had to shut down and send students home due to the coronavirus pandemic. Much to the dismay of parents who were required to take on the responsibility of teaching their children without any preparation. This book serves as a guide for parents who are concerned about the next crisis or simply want to have control over their children's education.

Before starting homeschooling, parents must get familiar with the following: laws governing their state; benefits of joining a homeschool group; space needed to homeschool; how to set goals and scheduling; socialization possibilities; extracurricular activities; curriculum choices; how to tailor the curriculum to match each child's learning style; standardized tests options; portfolio requirements; choosing a school for classes parents are not equipped to teach; understanding accreditation requirements; EOC (End of Course) tests; dual enrollment; university requirements; support groups; homeschool costs; and the importance of family support. Don't PANIC! I know this seems like the world's longest to-do list, but you can do it! Just stick with me. I discuss all these topics throughout the book.

COMPARING HOMESCHOOLING WITH BRICK-AND-MORTAR SCHOOLS

Although the majority of parents may not possess a college degree in education, test scores confirm that homeschoolers outperform students attending traditional schools taught by degreed professionals.

Numerous studies show that homeschooled students' testing scores are higher than their public schooled peers. For instance, a nationwide study performed by Brian Ray and published by Academic Leadership Journal (nheri.org) claims, "Homeschool students' achievement test scores are exceptionally high. The mean scores for every subtest (which are at least in the 80th percentile) are well above those of public school students." Parents' dedication seems to notably outscore specialization.

Why did we decide to homeschool our children? Although there are some benefits to attending public schools, it was a very frustrating experience. School was not challenging; misbehaved children got all the attention; homework assignments were counterproductive; lessons were repetitive; and the idea of "labeling" students was troublesome. I discuss these topics elsewhere in the book, but here is a synopsis.

- School was not challenging enough, so I had to supplement my sons' education. Both had more academic potential than they could demonstrate in a school setting. Although they were placed in "advanced" classes, it was still uninspiring. They completed classwork in one-fourth the time allotted by the teacher and had to sit quietly while classmates finished their work. My older son begged to be homeschooled, because he felt that school was a waste of time. Teachers tend to pay attention to students who are struggling and ignore overachievers.

- Misbehaved children become the focus of attention and occasionally teachers punish the entire class for the misdeed of one student. Public school teaching strategies do not encompass accelerated learning methods and students get in trouble because they are bored. Although there are many reasons for children to misbehave, not accommodating their learning pace is an issue. Students, who are able to retain information at a faster rate, often stay idle until the teacher is ready for the next topic, leading to frustration. Chapter seventeen goes over tried techniques that can be used to modify a child's behavior. It addresses the importance of focusing on children who are following instructions, instead of the ones who are acting out because they crave attention.

- Teachers do not have time to design thoughtful homework that would benefit each student, so they tend to assign busy work. Homework is also used to cover required content prior to mandatory assessment tests. Often, my sons could not participate in Cub Scout meetings or soccer practices because they had hours of busy work.

- Although the No Child Left Behind Act was meant to set high standards, I found no correlation between test results and curriculum improvement. Once students finish their exams, teachers begin concentrating on material required for the upcoming year's test. I cover this topic in more detail in chapter seven and explain why monetary incentives given to schools force teachers to "teach to the test." Homeschool parents, on the other hand, use test results to improve lesson plans. I used assessment tests to create a curriculum that met each of my children's individual needs. Although standardized tests have their flaws, they can identify strengths and weaknesses we may overlook. Improving the curriculum, based on test scores, would be difficult in the school setting because teachers are often overwhelmed. Accommodating everyone's needs would be unmanageable.

- Schools are unable to customize teaching strategies to each student and rarely account for students' preferred learning style.

- The school system and some charter schools adopted curriculum that uses the spiral approach; consequently, students who do not require repetition are demotivated when schools use this method.

- Should all students be labeled? Teachers may label students gifted, with learning disabilities, behavioral issues, or food intolerant. As new labels emerge, I question the expertise of these child-labelers. Although some of these labels are placed to get students the assistance they need to succeed in school, others just hurt students' chances of progressing academically. For example, based on assessment tests, students may be labeled as bright, average, or strugglers. The brightest students are given advanced material, while struggling students are assigned lower-level work. At a public school the children I worked with who were labeled "struggling students" were placed in lower-level classes. Tests showed that their reading and math skills were not up to par with their peers.

Although there is a system in place to identify students' academic levels and a sense of urgency in providing a label, there is no guideline to remove it. These students progressed so rapidly that within a few months they surpassed the advanced students' skills. I did not need a test to confirm their improvement; however, tests were mandatory to move them to higher-level classes.

There is nothing wrong with having students work at their skill level based on test results; however, by the time teachers find time to reassess their skills, students are bored and may have lost interest in learning.

Have schools considered the impact of labeling students? According to research conducted by psychologist Carol S. Dweck, Ph.D., if students are told that they are smart they work harder and that comment alone will change their attitude towards learning.

What message are we sending students who are placed in lower-level classes?

In the first few years of elementary school, children's development is uneven and idiosyncratic, and a standardized test may not be a good representation of their ability. They should be treated as unique individuals because they grow and mature at different paces. The truth is that the vast majority of public school students are lost in the massive wasteland of mediocrity.

Teachers are undermining students' abilities by placing labels and not reevaluating their skills in a timely manner. Do students need to be given a qualifier in order to get a good education?

The conventional school curriculum fails to stimulate students' hunger for knowledge. The combination of my sons' frustration with school and my concern that they would not live up to their full potential, made me realize that homeschool was the only solution to provide them with a superior education where they could thrive. Homeschoolers can work on subjects to the point of mastery, unlike school children who stop once the bell rings.

These are some of the reasons we decided that homeschooling was the best option for our family. Of course, bullying and violence in the schools were also factors. It was vital to act fast so they would not lose their passion for learning. Although they were attending an A+ public elementary school, the middle schools in our neighborhood were less than desirable. The breakdown of public schools and the prohibitive cost of a "good" private education only add to homeschooling's appeal.

When I first started homeschooling, I was unable to find books on homeschoolers' real stories complete with curriculum choices and examples of strategies that succeeded and failed. Instead, books available were mere guidelines with a listing of curriculum available and how to start homeschooling. Some exceptions were books describing what to teach at each grade level, such as *What Your Fifth Grader Needs to Know and What Your Sixth Grader Needs to Know*. Both were very helpful to me.

Homeschooling can be intimidating, due to the enormous amount of information and curriculum choices available. Regardless, being able to select my own curriculum made it extra appealing. I could cater to my sons' needs and learning styles, knowing that the outcome would only depend on the amount of effort our family put in. Although we were motivated primarily by academics, homeschooling proved to have countless benefits. Whatever the goal and motivation are for homeschooling, parents can offer children the best chance of reaching those goals by teaching them at home.

Oftentimes, parents are surprised I chose the homeschool path and claim, "I could never homeschool my children, because they would never listen to me." A parent's role is to teach children social skills and the teacher's role is to create a safe environment where children can excel. If children do not listen to their parents, would they listen to their teachers? Teachers do not have the responsibility to teach character development, but frequently find themselves having to deal with students who challenge their authority in the classroom. Some parents feel the responsibility for the social upbringing of their child should lie in the hands of teachers, but are often disappointed to find out that teachers do not have time to deal with student behavior issues.

HOMESCHOOLING DURING A PANDEMIC

Whether your family is considering homeschooling, trying to get prepared for the next crisis, or simply curious on how to take charge of your child's education, use this book as a reference.

While some parents refused to homeschool during the pandemic because it was too much of a burden, others happily took on this new role. Some schools offered remote learning; others told parents what to teach during daily one-hour Zoom meetings.

In reality, these parents did not have the "homeschooling experience." Homeschool parents spend a lot of time developing a worthwhile program and the transition does not happen overnight.

Putting this level of responsibility on parents during a crisis, where some are concerned about losing their jobs or getting sick, is just potentially problematic. Even though they did the best they could, most wish they had been more prepared. Here was an auspicious opportunity to teach children to be independent.

Is it appropriate to expect parents to jump in and start acting as an educator under such trying conditions? Parents were unprepared and frustrated, but in reality some of the frustration came from unreasonable requests from teachers. For example, a friend's daughter who is only 7 years old was requested to do a presentation using PowerPoint. The parent, who is a college-educated professional, believed it was so unreasonable that she prepared the slide show herself, hoping that this type of assignment would be the last. The teacher was so impressed with the result that she turned it into a weekly project and, in addition, requested a video of the students explaining the process of making the slide show. This is just an example of how unreasonable and unrealistic some teachers can be. Most homeschool parents would never assign that type of project to a 7-year-old, so the level of frustration is not the same. Homeschool parents choose what is appropriate, and there is no due date. When homeschool students are having a bad day, they can take a break and continue the instruction when they feel better.

Funny comments made by parents, on Twitter, during the pandemic:

"Dad, what is a synonym?" "It's a spice."

"Two weeks into homeschool and my 9-year-old already broke the world's record for longest amount of time sharpening a pencil."

"Don't forget to write the date on top of the page." "What day is today?" "I don't' know. I think it is Tuesday or July 1st."

"My 6-year-old says that she misses her teacher."

"If you see my boys locked outside, mind your own business. We are having a fire drill."

CHAPTER FIVE

HOMESCHOOL REQUIREMENTS

HOMESCHOOLING IS LEGAL IN ALL 50 STATES, although rules and regulations differ from state to state. States may or may not require parents to have minimum education, vaccination requirements, allow students to attend public school part-time, allow parents to hire a tutor or enroll in correspondence schools.

HOMESCHOOL LAW

Homeschoolers can initiate their homeschool journey at any time of the year and each state has different requirements. Home School Legal Defense Office's friendly website offers an interactive map with a breakdown of each state's law, listing of homeschool support groups for each state, and resources to help parents start homeschooling. HSLDA has protected homeschoolers' rights and helped families understand their constitutional rights for over 35 years.

Homeschool students are "official" homeschoolers once parents notify the district's school superintendent office of their intent to establish a home education program. Parents have to provide an annual educational evaluation demonstrating educational progress by having their child take a nationally normed achievement test; an evaluation by a psychologist with a valid and active license or a certified teacher is also accepted. The latter is a great alternative for special-needs students. Requirements vary from state to state. For example, the IOWA test, which we used for eight years, is an achievement test adopted by private schools. The FCAT, which is used by public school students, is also an option for homeschoolers. Homeschool students in Florida prefer the IOWA test instead of the FCAT because it allows them to be compared nationally to all private school students.

Why do most homeschoolers prefer to be compared to private school students?

Since private and public schools adopted different annual assessment tests, we can't compare students' scores using that data. Public school assessment tests cannot even be compared across states, since a variety of tests are used across the country. However, data from the National Center of Education Statistics shows that private school students score 3.1 points higher on the ACT test, which is used for college admissions, compared to public school students. In conclusion, homeschoolers prefer to be compared to students with higher test scores.

Homeschool groups offer tests at different locations; however, a certified teacher must administer them. The computerized score report and annual evaluation letter are sent to the student's address. In Florida, parents are not required to send test results to a government agency; instead, they can send an evaluation prepared by a certified teacher that shows educational progress. If test scores are sent to the district's school superintendent and results fail to demonstrate educational progress, the superintendent notifies in writing that progress has not been achieved and offers parents one year to provide remedial instruction. After a year, the student has to be reevaluated and the continuation of a homeschool education is contingent on educational progress.

This book mentions Florida and New York homeschool laws; nevertheless, information on other states can be easily attained from the Internet. My favorite go-to site is HSLDA.com, which gives updated information on requirements for each state.

New York

Parents must file an annual declaration of intent with the local superintendent by July before starting homeschool. They have to file an individualized home instruction plan, maintain attendance records, submit quarterly reports, and conduct standardized tests.

Florida

Since 1985, Florida laws have protected home education. Parents are free to select their own curriculum. Students can learn at any location, any time of the day, and at their own pace. Florida Bright Future's Scholarship Program, which is a college scholarship, is also available to homeschoolers. Be aware that volunteering hours, which are a requirement to apply for the program, have to be approved by the district ahead of time. Notice of intent and a portfolio are required for most states.

A nationally normed student achievement test should be administered by a certified teacher once a year and a letter of termination sent to the school district superintendent office if homeschooling is concluded.

Notice of intent

A homeschool notice of intent is used to inform the department of education that your children will not be attending public or private schools and will be homeschooled instead. The letter should contain each child's name, birth date, and grade. Each state has different guidelines, but some require information on who will be the teacher. Although there is no official form, local homeschool groups can assist with a sample notice of intent. The intent must be filed with the school superintendent's office within 30 days before homeschool education starts and should be sent certified mail. Thirty-one states require to be notified prior to starting homeschooling.

Portfolio

The purpose of a portfolio is to provide a complete picture of the homeschooler's educational choices. It is required by most states, including Florida. The portfolio should document student's education choices and educational progress; in addition, it should contain samples of schoolwork for all subjects for each school year. Folders should be labeled for each subject, available for inspection upon 15 days' written notice, and preserved for two years. A few states require parents to send a portfolio along with a report in lieu of a standardized test.

> *Portfolios are not required in Montana, but I think it is valuable for me to keep some of the materials in case there is ever accusation of neglect. Also, it is fun for us to look back to see what we've done.*
>
> **J.E. (Polson, Montana)**

Even if a portfolio is not a requirement in your state, universities may request it for college admission. It is also beneficial for homeschoolers who are planning to return to a brick-and-mortar school. Information added to the portfolio (I suggest keeping everything in an accordion file or three-ring binder) might include:

- Copy of the table of contents from each book studied, summary of subjects covered during the school year, homeschool calendar, and attendance report.
- Samples of student' work throughout the year for each subject.
- Extracurricular activities: List of field trips, sports teams, educational travel (including photos, flyers, and memorabilia). Reports written for each trip, if available.
- List of reading material and educational videos.
- Description of projects and achievements.
- Optional: We added a copy of the novel my son wrote and all the Boy Scout awards.
- Parent-prepared transcript. (A transcript is a document that describes what courses a student completed, along with grades and GPA.)

Each state has its own requirements, so it's important to research if your state requires completion of an annual form.

Annual evaluation

An annual evaluation is required to be sent to the superintendent's office before the one-year anniversary date of submission of the letter of intent. The superintendent's office does not always require student test scores to be sent to them. An evaluation by a certified teacher concluding that the child has progressed at their grade, a national student achievement test administered by a certified teacher, a psychological evaluation, or any other method mutually agreed upon between the parents and the superintendent's office will meet this requirement.

STRICTEST STATES TO HOMESCHOOL

Although homeschooling is legal in all 50 states, the degree of freedom homeschool families have varies from state to state.

Georgia

Although not as restricted as other states, still not as flexible as Florida. Parents can teach any time of the year. Attendance record needs to be submitted once a month. Classes need to be held daily for four to five hours. Progress report needs to be generated for each student and kept for a few years, in case the superintendent requests it.

Massachusetts

Curriculum, including textbooks and workbooks, should be submitted for approval.

New York

The school board determines subjects that need to be covered and homeschool parents need to submit a detailed instruction plan, including textbooks and choice of curriculum. Attendance needs to be logged, indicating 180 hours of instruction each year. Parents need to submit a quarterly report, including assessment test results. Homeschoolers need to be tested every other year (fourth through eighth grade) and once a year for high school students.

North Dakota

While most states do not verify parents' qualifications, North Dakota requires that parents have a high school diploma or a GED. Otherwise, the state monitors the student for three years. They also monitor standardized test scores. Students are now allowed to learn outside of the home.

Ohio

The school district makes homeschooling difficult, even though the state regulations are not stricter than other states. The school district requires homeschoolers to fill out forms not required by the state. They also have the right to approve or deny the homeschool curriculum chosen by parents. It is required that a homeschool parent has a high school education or hires someone with a bachelor's degree to work with the student.

Pennsylvania

Yearly notarized affidavit for each student is required. Subjects need to be taught in English. Immunization and medical services are required. No one involved in the student's day-to-day activities can have been convicted of criminal offenses within the past five years. The annual evaluation should be done by a licensed psychologist or state-certified teacher.

Rhode Island

Regulation can vary from district to district. Unlike Florida, where parents only need to send a letter of intent when they first start homeschooling, the state of Rhode Island wants parents to submit the letter each year. The school committee has to approve the curriculum and timeline of all subjects covered. This is absurd! This would be no different than going to a public school, where the teacher needs to move onto new topics even if children do not understand a concept because they have to cover everything the state mandates. Staying on a topic until the concept is mastered is one of the biggest advantages of homeschooling. However, since parents have to turn in number of days each subject will be taught, there is no room for flexibility. Standardized tests, quarterly reports, and vaccination may be required depending on your district.

Vermont

Homeschoolers in Vermont need to learn no less than 12 subjects, with an in-depth outline of what will be taught submitted to the school board. This takes away from the benefits of homeschooling.

Please check your local Department of Education's website for more information on your state's requirements.

HOMESCHOOLING SPACE

It is important to provide an environment conducive to studying. Invest in a whiteboard, wall map, and computer(s). Classes can be held at a designated homeschool room, where all the children work together. We started with my children working in their rooms, eventually though I felt that they were too isolated, and we decided to set up an area in the living room for work to be done together. Lighting should be suitable and each child should have a comfortable chair. For students who cannot concentrate when it's noisy, earplugs help block out sound. An agenda should be provided and students can use Google Calendar to keep track of important due dates. Please note: Homeschool does not always have to be at home. Schoolwork can be completed at a local park, beach, museum, or any other public place.

FINANCIAL EXPENDITURE

Homeschooling costs depend on a variety of factors. Parents can be resourceful and borrow material from the library, sign up for free virtual school classes, get lesson plans from the Internet, buy used curriculum, or exchange curriculum with other homeschoolers. Even if parents choose to register their children in free online programs for main classes, they can still teach all the electives.

Curriculum fairs permit parents to examine curriculum thoroughly before buying. I revised material owned by my veteran homeschool friend to determine if her curriculum choices would work for us. Never feel obligated to purchase on the spot and be wise with your selection; there will be other opportunities. Read reviews online and select curriculums that are best suited to each child's learning style, deliver a quality education, and provide structure for your homeschool program.

There are hundreds of websites with free worksheets and interactive games. Starfall is an interactive website geared to young learners (chapter nine) and Only Passionate Curiosity offers free printable worksheets and a list of free curriculum organized by subject.

FAMILY SUPPORT

Family members may be skeptical about your decision to homeschool; however, only time will show your critics that their concerns were unwarranted. There is no need to solicit everyone's opinion because you do not homeschool to please others.

A supportive spouse is essential and it would be difficult to homeschool without his or her consent and support. The parent who decided to homeschool usually wants to be in control, so relinquishing even a small portion of the responsibility may be difficult. Other parents, however, may want one spouse to be more involved. Spouses can be involved by reading stories, having book discussions, teaching one of the classes, or helping with a co-op class.

My husband taught American History, read bedtime stories, was a leader for the Scouts, camped with our sons once a month, and travelled with us as much as his work schedule allowed.

Neighbors and friends also may have a strong opinion regarding your decision to homeschool; however, that should not be a factor in your judgment. People who didn't even know us and had no business having an opinion criticized us. Our friends and family were always supportive, and my husband was my number one supporter.

CHAPTER SIX

HOMESCHOOL REGIMEN

Having a schedule is a way to ensure students start school at a specific time and complete tasks assigned for that specific day. A schedule is essential to guarantee that short- and long-term goals are met. However, it is important to be flexible and change the schedule, if necessary. We homeschooled four days a week for six hours a day and had plenty of breaks for playing basketball, running around, or just relaxing. Once a week they had physical education with a professional homeschool program all day at a local park, along with hundreds of other homeschool children. City parks offer a range of sports throughout the year. I divided their schedule into week A & B and week C & D.

Language arts, mathematics, foreign language, science, and history were taught daily. The first two weeks of each month they learned writing, presentation, music, and grammar. The last two weeks I covered geography, which included virtual trips, as well as civics, cursive, typing, and art.

Both boys played competitive soccer at a local park a few times a week and a private tutor taught them how to play guitar once a week.

Boy Scouts of America gave my sons the opportunity to develop various skills: leadership, cooking, lifesaving and emergency preparedness, environmental science, personal fitness, personal management, swimming, and hiking. Scouts are required to earn a minimum of 21 merit badges (out of 130) to achieve Eagle Scout ranking. The intention is to guide, encourage, and expose scouts to different skills and assist them in finding the right career. Since my sons each took the college entrance exam at age 14, knowing what career to pursue was beneficial.

Make sure to add physical education, extracurricular activities such as dance or music, field trips with homeschool groups, and educational TV shows to your schedule.

Use a planning book to organize academic schedules for each subject. Our family set aside a specific part of the day for academic work.

Integrating all these extra activities into the curriculum is a smart way to create a lifestyle of educational questing. Incorporate subjects slowly, so students aren't overwhelmed.

HOW MANY HOURS OF HOMESCHOOLING ARE NEEDED?

Before we talk about how many hours of homeschool are needed, let's analyze how many hours school kids spend learning each day. School usually starts at 8 a.m. and ends at 2:50 p.m., varying from school to school. Fifteen minutes is used for announcements in the morning and taking attendance. Five minutes to switch classes, 10 minutes for recess, and 50 minutes for lunch. If students finish a lesson early, they might sit idle for 15 minutes. This can add up to 45 minutes or more a day. Let's figure an average of 15 minutes travel time to and from school each day, that adds up to 150 minutes of non-academic time each week. Normally, students go to school for six-and-a-half hours a day (390 minutes). Deducting non-academic time, school children have about four hours of academic work a day. From this calculation, one may argue that if homeschool students study from 8 a.m. to 12 noon, they attain better education than their school peers due to the one-on-one instruction.

In fact, a number of homeschoolers follow this rule. However, I wanted my sons to excel academically and the bare minimum was not an alternative. Consequently, our solution was to homeschool from 8 a.m. to 3 p.m. every day except for Thursdays, when they went to PE all day. This totaled six hours a day excluding lunch and breaks.

A total of 24 hours of academic work a week compared to 20 hours for traditional school students. Keep in mind that I did not account for all the time the teachers waste with misbehaved students. School system calendars show a total of 171 school days after removing teacher planning days, early release, and holidays. Since homeschool parents do not take time for planning days or early releases, their calendar totals 180 days of school per year. From this calculation, which of course can vary from school to school, homeschoolers received

864 academic hours compared to 680 hours for campus-based students. School children complete their homework in one to three hours, where homeschoolers have free time. Homeschool is also more efficient because students have individualized attention and there are no distractions.

LEARNING ON THE ROAD

Homeschool offers great opportunities to learn outside the home. The freedom to travel any time of the year is one of the best benefits of homeschooling. We can participate in field trips with other homeschoolers, read or study at the beach, or go to local parks to observe nature. Field trips are an effective educational tool that can be exceedingly rewarding compared to formal educational settings.

Zoo Miami, St. Augustine, Disney parks, Universal Studios, Cape Canaveral, state parks, beaches, museums, theaters, laser tag, mining, chess club, and paintball are field trips we took during the school year. What a privilege to have my sons at home and aid them to grow into the young men they are today.

Field trips

One of our favorite field trips was to Solid Waste Management in Palm Beach, Florida. It may sound strange; however, the learning opportunity was remarkable. This trash and recycling facility is a producer of renewable energy. While SWA's Renewable Energy facility reduces the volume of waste disposed of in the landfill, it also uses household trash as fuel to produce clean electricity. Waste-to-energy plants improve air quality since consumption of fossil fuels such as coal, natural gas, and oil goes down. Another alternative to fossil fuels, methane gas is generated from the landfill and exploited as a renewable clean energy. Using landfill gas, SWA is making one state-of-the art, environmentally beneficial project even better. At SWA's Biosolids Processing facility, landfill gas is applied to power sludge dryers as an alternative to natural gas. Sludge from wastewater treatment plants is dried up and sold as a natural fertilizer. SWA also has a recycling program for plastic, glass, aluminum, and paper. We spent a few days learning about recycling, fossil fuels, and fertilizers before our field trip to ensure a better learning experience. We also used these topics for our compositions.

Disney and Universal Studios on a budget

We visited Walt Disney and Universal Studios once a month in the middle of the week. Even though people perceive Disney as entertainment and not educational, our family managed to find instructive opportunities. For example, my sons learned facts on 11 countries by visiting Epcot Center. I created lesson plans on each country's history, allowing us to have discussions while exploring the park. Tasting ethnic foods and desserts from each country was a remarkable way to experience other cultures and their cuisine. Science can also be learned when visiting Disney. For example, children can learn about the relationship between gravity, mass, and distance during a roller coaster ride.

Allow children to observe the shape of Disney Cruise ship hulls, which are carefully designed to reduce drag. Plan a lesson on electricity with emphasis on source, watts, and load before going on rides. Observe millions of light bulbs throughout Disney and explain the importance of electricity, which enables all rides to function. Newton's Three Laws of Motion can be observed in every Disney theme park ride. Learn the differences between potential and kinetic energy: A roller coaster builds up potential energy during its initial climb and then releases it as kinetic energy when it races downhill. The Rock 'n' Roller Coaster can be explored to explain the magnetism and magnets used in audio speakers. Research magnetic fields and electromagnets by borrowing a book from the library, and find out how speakers work.

Develop lesson plans to investigate the science behind amusement park rides. Include YouTube videos to make it more engaging. Visual communication is one of the most effective ways to retain information.

Zoos and state parks

There are learning opportunities at zoos and parks. Study about animals and their environments. Nature, ecology, biodiversity, and adaptations are topics that can be explored at a zoo or park. Identify the differences between mammals, reptiles, and insects. Animals come from different parts of the world, so use this opportunity to teach geography and explain why certain animals can only be found in certain regions. Understand the definition of tundra, savanna, and rain forest. Have each child research his favorite animal and share with siblings.

Building a rocket

Travelling and field trips are not the only learning opportunities. Students can learn how rockets and Newton's Third Law of Motion come together by building a simple rocket using a bottle. Combining distilled vinegar and baking soda creates an acid and base reaction producing bubbles of carbon dioxide gas with enough pressure to launch a rocket.

This is not exactly a spacecraft launch lifting off and escaping Earth's gravity; nevertheless, it is an incredible simulation that imitates the chemical reaction used to send spacecraft into space. Newton's Third Law of Motion says that for every action, there is an equal and opposite reaction. The initial action is the rush of matter and force downward from the bottle's opening; the reaction is the bottle moving upward. Children should have an adult present to assist them when building and launching this rocket.

Dissecting preserved specimens

Dissecting provides hands-on experience in learning anatomy and allows students to explore animal organs and discover how tissues and organs interconnect. Many of the organs from animals are similar to those of humans. In addition, students can learn about the ecosystem and adaptation. As an example, some frogs are able to catch insects with their sticky tongue because of its speed, length, and strength.

Our family purchased a complete dissection kit with nine preserved animal specimens, tool set, dissecting pan, and instructions. You can also watch YouTube videos for guidance. One of the specimen's included was a cow's eye. It was intriguing to learn how a cow's eye muscles are attached to the eyeball and how that compares with our eyes. Humans have six muscles attached to their eyeball. Ask your children to move their eyes in all directions and explain how they differ from cows, which only have four muscles to control their eyes. As your children move their eyes in all directions, explain how cows cannot roll their eyes as humans can. (For parents of teenagers who always seem to be rolling their eyes at you, this can be perceived as a benefit.) Feel around the eye and understand how the eye muscles touch the surface of the eye (cornea), which helps protect the eyes. The pupil opens wide in the dim light, letting plenty of light in. The cow's pupil is oval, while the human's pupil is round. Remove the cornea and the  iris to observe the lens. Note that cow irises are always brown, while human irises can be green, blue, or brown. Cow lenses are shaped like the lens of a magnifying glass, similar to the human eye. The retina, attached to the back of the eye, contains light-sensitive cells that detect light. The optic nerve sends information from the retina to the brain. Unlike humans, cows have a tapetum behind the retina, which is a reflective layer of the choroid that helps with night vision by reflecting light back through the retina. This is an example of how detailed dissecting can be and what a wonderful learning tool it is to draw similarities with human organs.

The Home Science Tools website (HomeScienceTools.com) has all the tools needed for dissecting. Kits contain various types of preserved animal specimens, including a fetal pig, frog, perch, crayfish, earthworm, clam, starfish, grasshopper, or sea sponge.

Mining

 Gem and mineral mining in Franklin, North Carolina, started in the 1870s. Known as the "Gem Capital of the World," Franklin's mines are located in the heart of the Great Smoky Mountains. Our family mined there every summer for over 10 years looking for sapphires, rubies, amethysts, moonstones, topaz, quartz crystals, and occasionally Native American pottery. My sons' favorite mine is Rose Creek Mine, which is one of the three state licensed gem mines in Macon County,

North Carolina. Dig your own dirt, wash the dirt in a flume, and cross your fingers there's a gemstone left behind.

All these field trips and backyard explorations offer ample opportunities to explore nature and science and can accommodate all learning styles. Auditory learners will appreciate listening to zoo-keepers talk about various animals and their environment. Historians at national parks tell stories about the Civil and Revolutionary wars. The interactive aspects of these trips are a benefit for the kinesthetic learner. Visual learners benefit by reading descriptive signage. Tactile learners love exhibits that can be touched, whether it is the shed skin of a snake or bird feathers.

Skewed view of reality and a trip that changed my children

People may have an unrealistic view that by homeschooling their children, they will be isolated. Homeschoolers have countless opportunities to engage outside the home. Travelling is part of many homeschoolers' routines; they are free to explore the world around them, unhindered by the restrictions of their schooled peers.

By traveling and experiencing other cultures, homeschoolers get a panoramic view of the world around them. They notice nuances that a single viewpoint can't accommodate. Their perception of reality changes as they grow and their minds are open to new ideas because, unlike adults, they view the world without the weight of past experiences. As we grow, we are more reluctant to take on new challenges; however, different experiences shape kids into more confident adults. Adult preconceived notions should be put aside to allow children to see the world through their own eyes.

Children may have a slanted view of reality; astonishingly, it was extremely disconcerting when my sons complained about their perfect and stress-free lives. Our major concern in raising our sons was to ensure that they were not spoiled and ungrateful. They earned money by doing chores and could buy their own video games. I provided them with a list of chores and added a dollar value associated with each task, allowing them to work and earn money at any time. Since they earned their own money, they understood the value of each dollar and patiently waited until the latest video games went on sale before buying them. They always correlated how many windows or baseboard they needed to clean with how much they had to earn to buy a specific game. The only caveat was that they needed to complete certain chores without getting compensation, before earning money. We emphasized that they were part of the family and everyone needed to contribute.

I grew up poor and, like most other children, I complained about not having clothes or toys I believed I was entitled to. One day my mom decided to surprise my sister and me with a field trip. We put on our best outfits and were astonished when we discovered that our field trip was not an exciting day at the park or the beach; instead, we visited the slums of São Paulo, which are called "favelas" in Portuguese. São Paulo is the largest city in the Southern Hemisphere and although it is relatively prosperous, poverty is a colossal problem. Substandard housing occupies over 50 percent of the city. Thirty years ago, favelas lacked electricity and plumbing, which thankfully is not the case today. We walked up this unpaved road to an elderly woman's home. My mom had assisted this lady for a few years with food and other major necessities; consequently, she knew exactly where to take us when we complained about life. The lady had a one-room shack made from old recycled wood and corrugated metal. The dirt floor had that humid, musty smell, and there were no windows to alleviate the odor. A tiny bed was placed on uneven dirt, and there was a little table with wood chips under each leg to help level it so the propane stove on top wouldn't slide off. She used lanterns to illuminate at night. The toilet was simply a hole in the ground covered with a piece of wood, which served as a lid. The whole area was densely packed with tiny houses made of wood, cardboard, or corrugated iron. Some of the houses were made of concrete blocks, unfinished and unpainted. Unfortunately, the majority were half built since they could only afford to buy a few concrete blocks every month. Our mom wanted us to understand how fortunate we were to own a two-bedroom house for a family of five. She sure made her point, and my sister and I never complained again.

When my children were 10 and 12 years old, they were fortunate enough to have the opportunity to observe people living in poverty. Being poor in the United States is hardly the same as being poor in other countries. We travelled to Brazil almost every year and visited the North, South, and Central regions.

While in Rio de Janeiro, a driver who worked for the hotel informed us that tourists usually visited the favelas (slums) and he would be glad to take us on a tour. I remembered what a valuable lesson that had been for me, so we went to two different favelas in one day. The first was the favela do Alemão, where people rode a gondola to get to their house on the top of the hill. This aerial lift connects 13 different favelas (over two miles). My kids were able to spot children playing on their rooftops, since the houses have no back or front yard.

The second was favela da Roçinha. We walked through the narrow streets with dilapidated houses, shocked that people could live in such conditions. Because the streets are too narrow for cars, motorcycle taxis transport locals to their humble houses on the top of the hill. Electricity lines create giant webs on the poles, a free-for-all system, which is extremely dangerous and frequently causes these poor people to lose their houses to fire. This favela is home to over  a hundred thousand people. Children start working as early as 7 years old to assist their family by selling candy or washing car windows on the street corners. It was quite shocking and a BIG life lesson for my boys. They now have a unique perspective about life and know the difference between needs and wants.

Virtual field trips

Virtual field trips are often free and less time-consuming than real trips. There are ways to study and learn about various topics in an enjoyable way, just by having access to the Internet. (Websites come and go, so if you can't find the one you're looking for, there's bound to be another on a similar topic. Help your children search for a comparable site.) Virtual trips enable parents to take children to places all over the world at no cost and are a great way to supplement a curriculum.

The Colonial Williamsburg Foundation offers online field trips that feature historical documentaries, videos, live discussions, and even games. They offer live TV broadcasts about the Revolutionary War, the work of modern historians, the Civil War, and other historical happenings. These videos integrate history, technology, and science examples that correlate to national teaching standards. Students can send in questions and a historian will answer them.

The Smithsonian National Museum of Natural History offers a worthwhile panoramic virtual tour. Rooms can be viewed by clicking on specific buttons, which allow 360-degree and close-up views of objects and exhibits.

Panorama.dk website offers high-definition panoramas complete with historical facts from anywhere in the world, including the Seven Wonders of the World architectural monuments; Great Wall of China; Colosseum in Rome; Petra in Jordan; Machu Picchu in Peru; Taj Mahal in India; Christ Redeemer in Rio; and Chichén Itzá in Mexico.

CHAPTER SEVEN

SHOULD STUDENTS BE TESTED?

S CHOOL TEACHERS TEST STUDENTS TO MEASURE their understanding of content taught in class and prepare them for annual assessment tests for reading, writing, mathematics, and science. Standardized tests are a highly controversial topic.

The No Child Left Behind Act was created to set high standards and measurable goals to improve education. All public schools are required to provide an annual standardized test where students are expected to show continuous improvement year after year. Schools that show no improvement are given the label "In Need of Improvement." Teachers and administrators are under a lot of pressure and, as a result, quality of education took a downturn.

School districts hold teachers and schools accountable for the quality of education by comparing all the schools' performances and offering rewards to teachers who boost their students' tests score.

Teachers feel that putting too much emphasis on a single test prevents them from exploring new technologies and teaching methodologies. Parents argue that "teaching to the test" forces teachers to shape their instructions around the test and not concentrate on the content knowledge of each year's curriculum. As an example, when my children were in elementary school, the FCAT writing test was only offered to fourth, eighth, and tenth graders. The teacher vigorously worked with students all year preparing them for the fourth-grade-writing test. It was disappointing to find out that once the test was done, students would not learn more writing skills until eighth grade. In fifth grade, teachers would concentrate on the reading exam. Monetary incentive, offered by the state, directs teachers to concentrate on a specific body of content embodied by each year's test.

Some homeschool parents believe there is no need to test their children, feeling that the one-on-one contact is sufficient to evaluate progress without the need for quizzes or exams. Traditional tests, overseen by the school system, are not administered to provide feedback to students or augment teaching strategies. Homeschool parents, however, can use these tests to implement unique teaching strategies. Standardized tests also are used to compare student performance across the country. As a homeschooler, I found that testing was useful to compare my children's score with other students nationally to gauge if what they were learning was benefiting them or if adjustment to the curriculum was needed.

WHAT IS THE DIFFERENCE BETWEEN TESTING AND ASSESSMENT?

Although these terms are used interchangeably, the major difference is that assessment is used to develop and implement unique teaching strategies for future lessons. Testing, also known as summative assessment, surveys students' knowledge and results are construed to improve teaching plans and are usually administered after instruction.

Types of assessments

- **Summative assessment:** Typical graded tests and quizzes administered by teachers at the end of each lesson. Although it is important for homeschoolers to become accustomed to these tests, formative assessments are more beneficial and should be applied on a regular basis.
- **Formative assessment:** Identifies gaps and assesses how much students learned.
- **Diagnostic assessment:** Pre-test to identify previous knowledge. Can also detect areas that need reinforcement or intervention. Since there is no pressure associated with grade, this assessment is a true measure of a student's knowledge.

Homeschool students only take standardized tests once a year, typically to satisfy a state requirement. Testing can have value above and beyond simple compliance with the school district or to evaluate student progress. Parents can use formative assessment results as a tool to expose gaps and use results to develop necessary adjustments to the curriculum. The reality is that children only take full responsibility for course material if they are held accountable for it. Test taking, whether formative or summative, is a skill that needs to be perfected and can only be accomplished by doing it repeatedly. Allow a few weeks for students to study for a test and make sure that testing occurs often, so that they stay engaged.

Parents tend to come up with excuses when children underperform on a test, granting children permission to not apply themselves or work harder. If a test score is low, the child needs to spend additional time studying or parents may need to improve teaching strategies.

My children were given monthly formative assessment tests for math, vocabulary, comprehension, and science. Every few months, assessment tests were administered for civics and history. An alternative is to have discussions with children and assess progress in lieu of a traditional test or assessment.

Laboratory reports can be used to measure science progress. Science experiments augment understanding of scientific knowledge. Lab reports should include: Title, Introduction/Purpose, Materials, Methods, Data, Results, Analysis, and Conclusion. Although challenges inherent with science experiments are not usually part of a lab report, my sons included measurement errors associated with each experiment and troubleshooting methods related to equipment failure. They worked together on the same experiments, allowing them to discuss and collaborate on results. To enhance mastery of scientific facts, we would discuss the conclusions of each experiment before lab reports were generated and presented to the family.

Mandatory annual standardized test options

There are a variety of standardized tests to choose from; however, the Iowa test is the most popular in Florida. These tests are objective in nature and the process to remove bias is extensive. Along with the test scores, a homeschooler receives an evaluation form from a certified teacher. This form does not include test scores, it only highlights whether the student passed or failed the test. This is beneficial for parents who feel uncomfortable sharing test scores with the school system. Find out if your state requires standardized tests or if a certified teacher's evaluation would suffice.

Some students underperform because they have difficulty concentrating. One way to reduce children's stress is to let them understand that this test is *for mom*, to certify that *she* is teaching adequately. Standardized tests offer a snapshot of academic skills of a large sampling of students from the same grade level. There are innumerable standardized tests available including, Stanford, Iowa Test of Basic Skills, and California Achievement Test. These tests are a numerical and statistical indicator that aids school's admission to impartially compare candidates. A student's GPA is not a good gauge, since not all schools offer AP or honor's classes. Since these classes weight more heavily on the transcript, it would not be appropriate to only look at a student's GPA. Another issue is that there is subjectivity in the grading process, making it difficult to compare grades. So, standardized tests are considered the only objective gauge and statistical component common to all applicants.

STANDARDIZED TESTS (KINDERGARTEN TO HIGH SCHOOL)

Below are some common tests that can be used by homeschool students. Each test caters to specific grade levels.

Iowa Test of Basic Skills

This test compares student abilities across the country, from private schools to homeschoolers. It offers an opportunity for parents to drive and perfect curriculum decisions by evaluating how students are progressing in specific academic areas and use as a diagnostic tool to create intervention. Students are objectively and statistically compared to homeschoolers and private school students.

There are two types of Iowa tests: core and complete.

- The core Iowa test includes math and reading.
  The math test includes math computation, problem solving, and data interpretation. The reading portion includes usage and expression, vocabulary, reading comprehension, spelling, and punctuation.
- The complete Iowa test includes math, reading, social studies, science, maps and diagrams, and reference material.

Kindergarten through high school students can take the Iowa tests. A personal evaluation, performed by a certified teacher, is also accepted by the state of Florida and other states in the United States.

Iowa Test Practice Book

I highly recommend purchasing Iowa test practice books, especially if your children are taking this test for the first time. These books help familiarize children with the format and permit parents to assess which topics need added emphasis throughout the year.

We purchased the *Scoring High Iowa Tests of Basic Skills* book. It covered vocabulary, reading comprehension, spelling, capitalization and punctuation, usage and expression, math concepts and estimates, math problem solving and data interpretation, math computation, maps, diagrams, reference materials, and science.

The School Board in Florida requires proof of progress for language arts and math.

Analyzing the Iowa test score

The national percentile ranking on the Iowa test describes student performances from 1 to 99 compared to other students from the same grade. If students fall into the 75th percentile, that means they scored as well or better than 75 out of 100 students who took the same level Iowa test.

Grade Equivalent (GE) score: Student scores can range from 0.0 to 13+. For example, a 7.3 GE score indicates knowledge equivalent to a student in the third month of seventh grade. A sixth grade student with a 7.3 GE score would be above average, while an eighth grader would require remedial work.

Peabody Individual Achievement Test

The PIAT test is an oral standardized test that is individually administered by a certified teacher. It covers general information, spelling, reading comprehension, reading recognition, mathematics, and spelling. The test result, which is calculated after the exam, indicates grade level and percentile ranking. Although the exam is not timed, it normally takes from 60 to 90 minutes to be administered. The teacher tests students using questions at their grade level and works toward more advanced material until the student misses five to seven consecutive questions. At this point, the scholastic grade level is established.

A certified teacher performed my son's sixth grade annual evaluation. The results were off the charts (13+), showing results equivalent to seven grades above his grade level. Doubting the results, I signed him up for the Iowa exam to compare grades. To my surprise, results were similar on every subject.

Test results are sent to a student's home address and include computerized score reports broken down by subject and skill, which can be used for remediation. It also includes an evaluation letter, in case parents prefer to send the evaluation in lieu of the test.

The conclusion was that the Iowa and the Peabody Individual Achievement Test results were similar.

Should your child take the written Iowa test or the oral test?

Here are advantages and pitfalls of each choice:

- If a question is not clear during an oral exam, the examiner can clarify it.
- Questions can be adjusted and skipped if the examiner feels the student has not learned a specific topic. Before the teacher asked my son a question, she would ask if he learned the topic.
- The oral exam may take less time.
- A student's ability to expand on a topic is tested, which is a benefit for an extrovert and not an asset for an introvert.
- Grading can be based on the approach the student took in getting the answer and not necessarily on the correct answer, making the oral test subjective.
- Immediate feedback can be a benefit.
- Thinking aloud requires more concentration; however, oral exams may be an advantage for children who can be easily distracted.
- If the student is tired, the teacher may allow a small break. During a written exam, the examiner determines break time.
- A written test, in a classroom setting, may have distractions. A student with a nervous tic seated across from your child could be disrupting if the student is hissing, sniffling, or grunting. Although this can be avoided by taking the oral test, students should get accustomed to distractions since the one-to-one test is not always available.

Basic Achievement Skills Inventory Test

This test can be used for third to 12th graders. It covers vocabulary, spelling, language arts, math, and reading comprehension.

California Achievement Test

CAT is a nationally normed standardized test used for homeschooling and private schools. It measures achievements for language arts, math, and reading.

Comprehensive Test of Basic Skills

CTBS measures academic progress in pre-reading, spelling, reading, math, reference skills, social studies, and science.

Stanford Achievement Test (Stanford 10)

This standardized test was adopted by a number of schools, homeschoolers, and American schools abroad. It assesses students from kindergarten to 12th grade in reading, math, science, social studies, and language arts.

TEST-TAKING BENEFITS

Standardized tests provide a way to measure all students in a consistent way. Although some people believe that standardized tests should not be a requirement for children in elementary or middle school, test-taking skills improve with practice, which benefits students in the future.

Most high schools require a standardized test entrance exam as part of their admission process. Universities require students to take the SAT or ACT exam to be admitted into an undergraduate program; GRE and GMAT for graduate programs; MCAT for medical school; and LSAT for law school admission. While an applicant's GPA is important, an "unweighted" GPA is the only way to compare students. High schools provide colleges with transcripts that have weighted and *unweighted GPA*. Although colleges do not use *weighted GPA* to compare students, honor and AP classes will reflect the rigor of the student's coursework. However, the SAT is considered a more valuable admission tool than GPA because it is the only dependable gauge that is common to all applicants.

Formative assessments can be used to detect skills not yet mastered. After receiving my children's test results, I would review the sections they needed help with and create lessons to cover those concepts. My younger son had difficulty with the Iowa test section on maps, diagrams, and reference materials. So, I purchased the *Scoring High Iowa Tests of Basic Skills* book and worked with him on those concepts. He received a perfect score on that section the following year. The same can be accomplished with other sections of the test.

OPTIONAL TESTS

Duke Tip Talent Search

Duke University's talent identification program (TIP) identifies seventh grade students who are scholastically gifted and provides them with resources and academic challenges not offered in the classroom. Lower grade levels can also participate; however, I feel that fourth and fifth grade students are too young and would not benefit from the program. Qualified homeschoolers can participate along with brick-and-mortar students. Public and private school students must be invited by their school to participate in the program, based on their standardized test scores. Homeschoolers, however, can apply for the program online as long as they meet standardized test scores set by the program. Candidates must take the SAT college entrance exam at a local school. Depending on their academic abilities, students can gain access to unique resources at Duke University or local universities. Test scores are removed from students' file, unless parents request otherwise. The ACT test measures what students learned in school, while SAT tests reasoning and verbal abilities. The SAT penalizes students for wrong answers; the ACT test does not.

Duke offers summer and online classes to motivate and enrich students' academic skills. These academically talented students are invited to participate in innovative programs provided by Duke University to support their optimal educational potential. Opportunities to participate in enrichment programs build up students' credentials and improve chances of getting accepted into a top university.

End of Course Assessment (Eoc)

Many states administer EOC tests to measure students' knowledge on specific subjects. In Florida, students can take elementary, middle, and high school classes through Florida Virtual School. Classes are free of charge and homeschoolers can choose to take one or more classes. Homeschoolers who sign up for American History, Algebra I, Civics, Geometry, or Biology classes at Florida Virtual School should schedule EOC tests offered by their assigned public school at the end of each class. These tests are a requirement for graduation in the public schools in Florida. My sons took the EOC test for Algebra and Geometry at a local public school, while still in middle school. Although this is not a requirement for homeschoolers, it is a good idea to take these tests if children have to reenter the school system due to unforeseen circumstances.

This happened to my family because of a car accident!

The End of Course test is a mandatory academic assessment, overseen by the School Board in Florida, Georgia, North Carolina, Mississippi, Missouri, and other states. Depending on the school, students are required to score a three to pass or a four for graduation eligibility. These tests assess students' content knowledge for each individual subject. Check with your school board for a list of tests required, since new tests are added each year.

CHAPTER EIGHT

CHOOSING CURRICULUM TO FOSTER INDEPENDENCE

PARENTS NEED TO USE GOOD JUDGMENT when defining what curriculum benefits each child. Homeschool groups are a great resource and parents depend on them for information and advice. However, they have no legal obligations to give advice on intricate aspects of the homeschooling law or what to teach each child. Although these organizations have each child's best interests in mind, as a volunteer organization they have no resources in place to guide or advise families on every issue related to homeschooling. Parents are the only ones in charge of their children's education, and it is their responsibility to make the best decisions for their family.

Choosing a curriculum is the most challenging and significant decision for homeschooling. Since we are not obligated to adhere to a specific curriculum in Florida, and there are literally hundreds to choose from, the biggest dilemma is figuring out which curriculum to choose and what to teach in any given year.

Consider each child's learning style before creating lesson plans or purchasing a curriculum. Nobody is better positioned than parents to discern their child's learning style. One of the primary advantages of homeschooling is catering to each child's needs. My younger is a visual and kinesthetic learner. He loves to read, prefers written instructions, learns by observing, and benefits by reinforcing lessons with videos. My elder son is an auditory learner. He can recall what he hears, follows oral directions, and does not have to take notes to learn. Both benefit from kinesthetic learning.

A kinesthetic learner needs to adapt to different environments. When my younger son was in elementary school, he had to constantly move around to aid with assimilation of information. Although this learning style is well known and accepted, he had to learn to quiet down during annual assessment tests or church services. Other than just telling him to wind down, I did not have any suggestions on how to help him adapt to these situations.

Now that he is an adult, he told me how he managed to compose himself and stay out of trouble. He used to suck on his thumb when he was little, and his dentist recommended a fixed orthodontic appliance to avoid serious damage to his permanent teeth and jaw. He distracted himself by playing with the spinner roller attached to the appliance in his mouth, which helped him quiet down. Unknowingly, he was using the tension and relaxation technique recommended by psychologists to help release tension. This technique involves tensing and relaxing different muscles. As he played with the roller, he was applying tension to the tongue, which is a muscle; then when he stopped, the muscle would relax.

When kinesthetic children are in a situation that limits their ability to move, they can use the tension and relaxation technique, breathing technique, or meditation. For children to adapt to long periods of quiet, a breathing game can help. A five-minute reflection with breathing exercises will increase self-control. This skill requires time and perseverance; nevertheless, it is fully attainable.

A number of curriculums have been planned and scheduled for homeschoolers. Some include supply kits and detailed instructor's guides that allow extra time for parents to teach. They are laid out with simple, easy-to-follow steps that allow children at different grade levels to use the same material. Build from scratch curriculum and virtual classes are also popular among homeschoolers. I found that the majority of homeschool materials were not in-depth and would not benefit my children academically. For that reason, I built some of our curriculum from scratch, bought off-the-shelf curriculum, and used accredited online schools for core high school classes.

GUARANTEEING NO EDUCATIONAL GAPS

Correlating state guidelines with the curriculum of your choice helps guarantee there will be no gaps in your children's education. Proper curriculum sequence provides continuity in case children need to return to the school system.

What to teach each school year

Before you plan which subjects to teach, obtain information on legal requirements for your state.

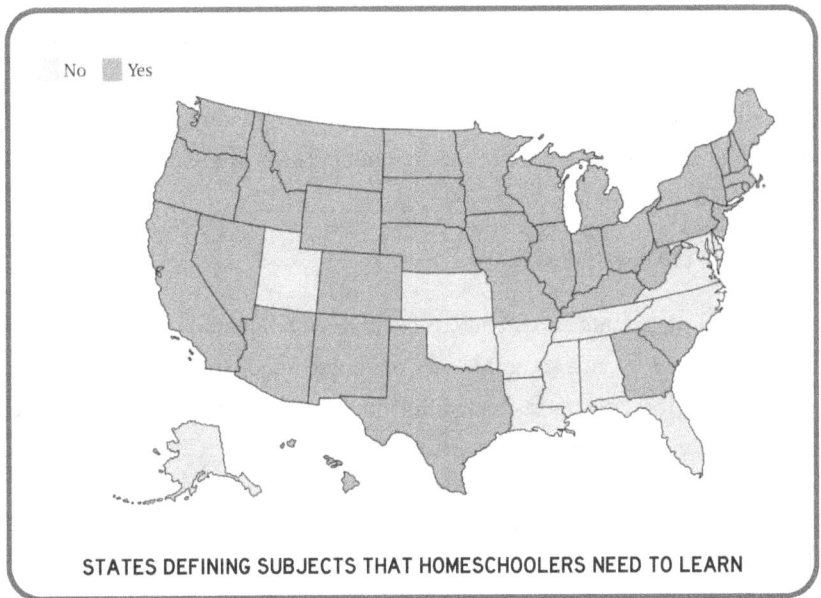

STATES DEFINING SUBJECTS THAT HOMESCHOOLERS NEED TO LEARN

Florida is one of 14 states that does not explicitly define what subjects should be taught, so parents have the freedom to choose what to teach each year. First, concentrate on core subjects (mathematics, English, science, and history) before worrying about electives.

New York State requirements or guidelines from other states can be used as a reference.

New York State explicitly defines which subjects homeschoolers should learn for elementary, middle, and high school.

a. First through sixth grade: Math, reading, health education, spelling, writing, English, science, geography, American History, music, physical education, and arts.

b. Seventh through eighth grade: English, mathematics, science, history, geography, health education, arts, music, and library skills.

c. Ninth through 12th grade: English, social studies (American History, civics, and economics), mathematics, health education, art, music, science, and electives.

These guidelines are just the basic requirements, and parents can add or remove some subjects if their state does not have subject requirements. We taught the core subjects and picked others that suited our children's interest, such as engineering.

Customizing your curriculum is one of the main benefits of homeschooling. Elementary and middle school classes are not as critical and should be selected to enable students to do well in high school. Although curriculum customization can be accomplished through high school, university requirements should play a role in determining course choices.

High school class requirements

Homeschooling parents have to determine high school graduation requirements, since most states do not set guidelines for homeschool students. Some exceptions are New York, North Dakota, and Pennsylvania. States, such as Tennessee, require students to either enroll with an umbrella school (Chapter 15) or take accredited online classes, which means parents do not get to set their children's high school requirements. However, most homeschool parents follow the same requirements of traditional schools. Public school students have an option to graduate with 18 credits; on the other hand, college-bound students should seek at least 24 credits to be competitive. Keep in mind that one credit is equivalent to 135 hours of study. Upon completion of these requirements, homeschool parents issue a high school diploma.

North Dakota, New York, and Pennsylvania are the only states that enforce high school graduation requirements to homeschoolers, according to Homeschool Legal Defense.

The following are high school graduation requirements for traditional school students in Florida.

- English Composition and Literature = 4 credits
- Mathematics (Algebra I and above) = 4 credits
- Science (plus two labs) = 3 credits
- Social Studies = 3 credits
- Foreign Language = 0 to 2 credits
- Fine Arts = 1 credit
- Health = ½ credit

- Physical Education   = 1 credit
- Electives   = 8.5 credits

A link to high school class requirements for all 50 states is on my website FromHomeschoolToHarvard.com.

Social studies classes can be American History, world history, economics, or American government. Foreign language is not a requirement for graduation; however, it is a requisite to receive scholarships and gain admission into most universities. Although the number of credits varies from school to school, most colleges require a minimum of two years of a foreign language. Stanford University requires three years minimum and Harvard four years. Students should take the same language all four years. Even if the university's requirement is two years, extra credits will strengthen the application. A bilingual student may be able to score a four or five on an AP exam to show proficiency in a second language.

Colleges do not stipulate which language students learn; however the chosen language should align with career goals. If English is not a student's first language, it is likely that he or she may not need to meet this requirement. Even if students are not college bound, follow the college prep guideline anyway, because teenagers are not mature enough to make that decision and may change their minds.

What is the next step after selecting classes for each student?

The difficult part after choosing the subjects is to create lesson plans. For children in different grade levels, find subjects that can be taught at the same time. My sons were two years apart; however, history, art, music, and some science were done together. Homeschoolers should learn at their level and not necessarily the grade levels that brick-and-mortar schools say they should be at. My sons were taking high school classes in sixth grade for math, science, and history. Even if you do not develop your own curriculum and decide to buy an off-the-shelf option, you can design your lessons and put together an eclectic mix. Consider your children's strengths and weaknesses. Try not to follow page by page and make sure to modify the curriculum to suit each child's needs.

Do not get hung up on grade levels, because homeschoolers accelerate at a much faster pace. Once I had a list of all the subjects I wanted to teach, the next step was to figure out what to teach from each book. Some subjects, such as math, require sequential learning. To ensure that there were no gaps in their education, I decided to correlate my lessons with state standards. At the time, Florida had adopted the Sunshine State Standards. These standards are meant to be used as a guideline and highlight what students need to learn at any given school year.

My technique was simple and effective. Correlation was done per grade and subject level, ensuring they learned the school's mandatory topics in addition to lessons from our curriculum. Step-by-step instruction on how to align to the Sunshine State Standards can be found on my website. The idea is to use state standards as a guide and not to replicate what brick-and-mortar schools teach. Only main ideas are identified, and parents choose their own material, procedures, and instructional aids to cover each topic.

The most common standard in the country is Common Core State Standards, which was created in 2010 to bring the education systems of all states into alignment. However, nine states opted out and created their own standard, because the Common Core curriculum did not guarantee high-test scores and was not tailored to meet each state's diverse needs. Florida adopted the Common Core curriculum for a few years and then changed back to the Sunshine State Standards.

Regardless of which standard your state adopted, all standards are designed to identify and create high-quality education. The goal is to ensure that all students are prepared to complete their upper education successfully and are career-ready.

Aligning your curriculum with state standards

CPALMS website is a platform for educators and parents that offers an interactive tool to help implement teaching guidelines. It provides access to the standards and course descriptions for all subjects for each grade level.

Sunshine State Standards offer instructions and resources for K-12 in the following subjects:

- Core subjects homeschool parents need to cover: English language arts, English language development, health education, mathematics, science and social studies (American History, geography, economics, civics, and financial literacy).
- Subjects that qualify as extracurricular activities: dance, music, foreign language, theatre, visual art, and so many more.

Homeschool parents can use the CPALMS website to search for guidelines for each standard. The same standard is sometimes used for multiple grade levels, so the lesson plan can include children from different grades. Obviously, the same standard at a higher-grade level is more in-depth and parents should take that into consideration when teaching a younger child. I only correlated my curriculum for the core subjects, excluding math.

The school system adopted the spiral approach where the same material is repeated year after year, but with increased depth. A homeschool parent, who chooses the mastery approach, may cover a topic all at once and work on a different topic the following year. (You'll find more information on mastery versus spiral approach in chapter two.)

Methods to find lesson plans

CPALMS's resource center can be used to find complete lesson plans, educational games, and videos related to each specific standard.

Searches can be by subject or grade level. Lesson plans, videos, and interactive lessons can be found on the website. Additional lesson plans can be found on the Internet for that specific standard. Videos and games are a great way to enhance your children's learning experience. My website has step-by-step descriptions on how to align curriculum topics with each state's standard and includes website links to each standard by state.

The same method can be accomplished with other standards chosen by your state. The only states that chose not to adopt Common Core Standards are: Alaska, Florida, Indiana, Minnesota, Nebraska, Oklahoma, South Carolina, Texas, and Virginia.

Determine the required material to be taught and link those lessons with topics found in the table of contents of the homeschool book you're thinking of purchasing. Although it is not recommended, it is possible to develop lesson plans based on state standards without a curriculum. I chose to develop my own curriculum and purchase some. Align and highlight state standards with lessons on your curriculum and enter those lessons into your yearly schedule. It should take four months to complete all topics required by the public schools, since homeschool parents can cover the material at a faster pace. Individualized attention allows parents to spend the rest of the year tackling advanced materials, expanding on topics of interest, or starting a new school year. The right academic decisions undoubtedly keep each child's welfare in mind.

Besides aligning my chosen curriculum topics with the Sunshine State Standards guidelines, I also aligned with the Core Knowledge guidelines. Core Knowledge is used in 750 schools throughout the United States. While the Common Core Standards provide a guideline on what to teach each year, Core Knowledge outlines how to teach. I purchased the books What Your Fifth Grader Needs to Know, and What Your Sixth Grader Needs to Know. These books recommend content for English, history, geography, visual arts, music, science and technology, and mathematics by grade level. Although topics for the first four months are similar to traditional schools, parents still have freedom to make pedagogical decisions that will benefit each child's individual needs.

Benefits of following this method

Aligning your lessons with public-school standards provides homeschool parents peace of mind and guarantees that students are learning exactly what they are expected to know at each grade level. Also, if there is a need for children to return to school, they will be ready academically. Most parents enter the homeschool journey thinking that it is a lifelong commitment. Life circumstances can change, and children may be forced to switch to a traditional school. Following these basic strategies helps ease the transition. Keeping a portfolio is also helpful, since some school counselors may require one.

Unfortunately, my sons were forced to make this transition after I was in a serious car accident and unable to homeschool them for a few years. They were ahead academically, and the transition was easier because we used this method. I was also glad we had kept a detailed portfolio since school officials eagerly looked through each folder.

TEACHING DIFFERENT AGE GROUPS

Homeschool parents need to be prepared for their children's developmental milestones, especially in middle school years when they endure emotional, intellectual, and physical changes. Curriculum and activities should be developmentally appropriate. As they grow, they question logic and demand consistency. Be ready for profound questions and use this opportunity to develop communication skills. State standards tend to repeat, so create lesson plans where the content is accessible to children from different grades. Design lessons for the older child and remove inappropriate sections of the content for younger siblings. If lessons cannot be combined, plan to teach one child while the second student is taking a test or working on an assignment. Since our language art curriculum was novel based, it was easy to tailor questions and activities to each of my son's abilities. It was a privilege to assist my children harness the inherent traits of each stage of their lives and build knowledge and character that will last a lifetime.

Curriculum choices

The ease and security of having a prepackaged curriculum is tempting, making it a simple decision for parents. Even though I purchased a few ready-made curriculums, I did not feel obligated to follow every page and each lesson.

Using technology to enrich your homeschool program allows subjects to come alive, especially for visual and reluctant learners. With the proliferation of educational software, which has taken over the market, there are vast options to choose from. Modern technologies guarantee interesting and entertaining learning experiences. The correct curriculum choice coupled with videos, virtual tours, educational computer programs, and educational shows will enhance your children's education. Books, magazines, and educational videos offer a wealth of information and are readily available at your local library.

Educational games and role-playing are effective and pleasurable ways to learn. Parents who lack certain expertise in a specific area can enroll their children in a correspondence school, virtual public school, or dual enrollment classes.

I preferred curriculum where children were able to complete a significant amount of work on their own because they need to learn to be independent at a young age. It is also beneficial to have assignments that can be completed without guidance for those days that one of the students needs more assistance. Florida Atlantic University's Research Department wrote an article (see excerpt below) after my 18-year-old son, "CM," graduated with a bachelor's degree in Neuroscience and Behavior.

> *CM is well aware of the benefits his mother's tutelage gave him. "Homeschooling definitely had an effect on my attitudes and work habits," he said. "My mother was very thorough in creating a personalized and well-rounded curriculum for me. She also pushed me to develop one very important skill: the capacity to self-learn. That was the single most important ability I used to succeed in college."*
>
> Read full article in Appendix A

No matter what curriculum is chosen, it is important to instill a genuine inquisitive attitude and passion for learning. One aspect to keep in mind is creativity, which is born from curious minds. In schools, however, exploration appears to always be in the way of expediency, because teachers concentrate on structural thinking, which eradicates creativity.

Working with each child individually enables parents to capitalize on each child's strengths and build up his or her weak areas.

Consider the following before buying a curriculum:

- Have you determined each child's learning style?
- Did you select mastery or spiral approach for mathematics?
- Have you determined your budget?
- Do you know if your children would prefer books, interactive programs, worksheets, or online programs?
- How hands-on do you want to be? Some curriculums require parents to be more involved and others empower students to work independently. What is your preference?

Once you've answered these questions, you're ready to choose a curriculum. After reading about my curriculum choices and after conducting your own research, attend a curriculum fair organized by a local homeschool group. Hundreds of homeschool representatives attend these events each year. Spend time reviewing curriculum programs that are best suited to your children before attending these events, because the heap of options available is overwhelming.

Homeschool catalogs provide a deluge of information, and they are an extremely helpful source for homeschoolers. When I first started homeschooling, I would read each and every page of the catalogs to find the best curriculum, books, and projects for my children. Rainbow Resource Center catalog, which was my favorite, provides an abundance of information. This catalog allows search by subject for kindergarten through 12th grade for curriculum, lesson plans, test prep books, and games.

CHAPTER NINE

OUR CURRICULUM CHOICES FOR MATHEMATICS

MATH IS A SUBJECT THAT BUILDS on previous knowledge. Mathematics curriculum can employ spiral or mastery approaches. The spiral approach can be extremely repetitive year after year, while the mastery approach goes over a specific topic and is taught until that skill is mastered.

In a school setting, even when teachers are aware that students have not mastered the preceding skills and do not have the prerequisite to learn new math concepts, they are forced to move on. The main reasons are that teachers feel the material will be revisited the following year, because schools use the spiral approach. Since math builds upon itself, having gaps in concepts can be detrimental to students.

This is another advantage of homeschooling: parents can stay on topic until their children understand it. If a student is struggling and fails to comprehend how to solve a problem, the parent's obligation is to intervene and assist.

When my younger son was 9 years old, he returned from school discouraged because the math teacher expected him to solve 100 multiplications problems in less than one minute and he was unable to accomplish it. To determine if that was a realistic expectation, I decided to solve the problems myself. Since I barely made it, my assumption was that it was an unreasonable expectation for a third grader. I searched for an interactive math program for visual learners to improve his multiplication skills and speed. *Math Drill Express* by Math Matters is an inexpensive, entertaining, and interactive program made up of games that teaches math facts employing multiplication, division, addition, and subtraction. Problems were timed and presented in a random and methodical way, and my son's math skills improved. In fact, he started getting perfect scores on the Florida Comprehensive Assessment Test. The teacher was so impressed she purchased the program for her son.

The spiral approach is commonly used in brick-and-mortar schools, but I knew that method was not the best option for my sons, since they were already exposed to it during their elementary school years. They took a placement test, offered by Teaching Textbook, to determine what math course was appropriate for their skill level. Placement tests were available for math three through seven, pre-algebra, Algebra I, Algebra II, geometry, and pre-calculus. Teaching Textbook is a CD-ROM-based math curriculum, where lectures and problems are worked out on a whiteboard. The curriculum offers step-by-step solutions to each problem and full explanations for all the homework problems. This versatile curriculum works for all different learning styles. If a child needs additional explanation, dynamic visuals and auditory inputs are available. This curriculum fits perfectly with lower-level math; however, I needed to find an enhanced solution for higher-level math courses.

After extensive research, I was delighted to find Video Text Interactive. Unlike the spiral approach used by Teaching Textbook or traditional algebra courses, Video Text Interactive uses a straightforward mastery approach. I believe that repetition is beneficial to a certain point; however, if overdone, children can lose interest. If the goal is to hold a child's interest in a subject, I found that the mastery approach works best.

At first, it seems that the Video Text Interactive algebra course is expensive compared to other programs; however, it is less expensive in the long run since it also includes pre-algebra, Algebra I, and Algebra II. Other curriculums sell each course individually. In addition, the online version is significantly less expensive. Each algebra program module includes course notes, student work text, solutions manual, instructor guide with progress tests, and DVDs. The video lessons are around five to 10 minutes long.

My husband wanted to hold on to the modules, so that our sons could review forgotten concepts as they took higher-level classes in college. However, they finished all their college math courses without having to review one single concept. Since the program does not force students to memorize rules or formulas and there are no shortcuts, they retain mathematical concepts needed for higher-level classes.

The videos, which are part of the lessons, enhance a student's ability to understand concepts. The three-dimensional animation helps students visualize concepts that are difficult to grasp. Envisioning mathematical functions and how they relate to graphs in a three-dimensional approach is easily understood. In addition, this curriculum demonstrates how to use an extremely efficient method that appeals to visual and auditory learners.

It is recommended that parents watch the video with their children and be available to answer questions they may have. Eventually, students are able to watch the videos on their own and independently complete their work. I enjoyed watching the videos with my sons because the concepts were explained in a methodical way and the graphics were impressive. As an electrical engineer, I took algebra, calculus (I, II, and III), differential equations, matrix systems, and probability and statistics. Algebra is considered the arithmetic needed to succeed in all future math classes. Learning with Video Text Interactive made it so my sons did not have to struggle with higher-level math in college.

Two quizzes for each concept (A and B) are included. My sons would solve every odd-numbered problem in each lesson and then take Quiz A. Since this method teaches concepts by not memorizing formulas, fewer problems are needed. If a concept or question on the quiz is missed, re-watch the video and ask them to work on the odd problems followed by taking Quiz B. Since explanations offered in the video were so detailed and made concepts clear the first time around, they only took the second quiz twice. Administer quizzes the following day to ensure that students understood and retained recently learned mathematical concepts.

My sons were taught to analyze problems, work through them systematically, and translate word problems into mathematical language; this system worked because my sons learned to solve complex word problems. We never called the help line for assistance; however, they are available, if needed. My sons successfully learned pre-algebra, Algebra I and Algebra II (high school level) using this curriculum while in sixth and seventh grade. They were full-time university students by age 15, and after taking the math placement test, were placed in the trigonometry college class. My younger son was tutoring Algebra II to high school students when he was 14 years old and started working for the university's math lab when he was 15. I believe that this curriculum played a role in my sons' accomplishments!

IS MATH AN INHERITED ABILITY?

Dr. Dweck's book *Mindset, The New Psychology of Success*, stresses that a positive mindset is what drives students to work harder, while others give up. Students with a "fixed" mindset believe that they are born with a specific set of talent and are limited by those talents. When they feel they've reached their expected ability, they stop trying. Students with "growth mindset" believe that if a concept is challenging, it will provide them with an opportunity to expand their knowledge with no restrictions due to inherited ability.

A similar notion is shown in Geoffrey Colvin's book, *Talent Is Overrated*. He validates that success is a result of a focused effort to increase one's knowledge. Also, hard work can result in success and that inborn talent is only helpful when students first start learning a new concept.

A twin study, conducted by the National Institutes of Public Health Access in 2007, shows that genes account for 32 percent to 45 percent of mathematical skills at a young age, and individual effort accounts for 55 percent to 68 percent. A twin study shows that the variation is due to genetics, shared environment, or unique environment.

Today's expectations are higher than when we were in school. Calculus, for example, was considered a college class. Today, it is expected that students finish calculus before they apply to college to prove that they can handle higher-level classes.

Richard Nisbett, Ph.D., Distinguished Professor at the University of Michigan at Ann Arbor and also a prominent cognitive psychologist, reports in his book, *Intelligence and How to Get It*, that his research team was able to convince high school students who were struggling academically that intelligence is malleable and can be changed by hard work. Students are also in charge of changing how they learn. The results were pleasantly surprising; these students worked harder and earned higher grades. Genetics plays a role in human intelligence, perhaps not as big of a role as most people think. Dr. Nisbett's research indicates that culture, social class, and education also impact intelligence.

American high school students' math scores, during an international math competition, underperformed compared with other countries. In *Intelligence and How to Get It*, Dr. Nisbett explores how the educational systems of East Asian countries place more importance on hard work and not as much on inherent talent. He explains how the Japanese, Chinese, and Koreans excel at math compared to Americans. He emphasized that students in Japan attend school 60 extra days a year compared to American students. This may be even worse than originally thought because after removing teacher planning days, holidays, and noon dismissals from the total number of hours, we may be at an even greater disadvantage.

As discussed in chapter six (How many hours of homeschooling is needed?), homeschoolers do schoolwork 180 days a year for a total number of 864 academic hours, compared to 680 hours for a brick-and-mortar school. Since homeschoolers have one-to-one instruction, they are able to cover the same material as a traditional school's students in one-third the time.

Japanese students spend from 210 to 240 days a year at school; however, some days are spent preparing for annual school festivals, culture day, sporting events, and school excursions. Dr. Nisbett clarifies that if students in Japan underperform to their standards, they work harder.

HOW TO TURN EVERY CHILD INTO A MATH PERSON

Practicing math improves a student's understanding and affects math skills. Encourage students to spend time on math and provide them with a variety of problems on the same topic. Remember that teachers fail to account for their students' preferred learning styles because it would be impossible to create lesson plans to meet each student's needs. Provide children with the appropriate curriculum to accommodate his or her learning style. Understanding math concepts helps avoid gaps that could be detrimental in the future.

Reviewing math topics before attending class can provide children the confidence required to understand and enjoy math.

Parents, who depend heavily on overworked math teachers to help their children, will eventually come to the conclusion that they need to be involved. The school system has deprived these teachers of training needed to teach math or the material necessary to teach a range of children with different learning styles. It is our responsibility, as parents, to be aware of our children's needs and assist them.

Consider hiring a math teacher, who is better suited for the job, if you feel overwhelmed and uncomfortable teaching high-level math.

Here are techniques that may help with anxiety when learning math, thereby avoiding frustration.

- **Frustration:** Children get frustrated when they do not understand a concept; which results in an anxiety-provoking experience. Acknowledge children's smallest successes by praising them. Emphasize that preparedness for class, regardless if homeschooled or not, enables teachers to assist them in understanding the material.

- **Memorization:** Instead of memorizing rules, students should understand mathematical concepts. Although memorization can be applied when learning math, most formulas can be derived from the basic formulas. Of course, math facts learned in elementary school require a level of memorization. My children did not memorize the multiplication tables; instead, we used the mnemonic method, silly pictures, and stories. This method associates a picture with a silly story that helps guide students to learn multiplication facts. Learning multiplication with rhymes:

    "6 times 8 is 48, so don't forget to finish your plate." —**Heather F.**

    "6 times 7 is 42, and don't forget to tie your shoe." —**Kristin Q.**

- **Handwriting skill:** The majority of my younger son's math mistakes were due to sloppy handwriting; the teacher could not understand his writing, so partial credit was not offered. He worked on improving his handwriting by tracing over numbers when he was in elementary school.

- **Missed concepts:** Since math builds upon what students have already learned, assistance should be offered as soon as a problem is noticed.

- **Homework:** Math homework can be tedious and repetitive; yet, reinforces skills learned at school. However, children do not need hours of homework.

- **Challenging concepts:** If students are having difficulty with a specific concept, encourage them to work on extra problems related to that idea.

- **Word problems:** Learning to solve word problems and converting numbers into words can be challenging. The step-by-step approach used by Video Text Interactive helped my children solve any type of word problem. Help students identify key words and which math operation applies to each problem. For example, words for subtraction may be "decreased by," "less than," and "take away." "Product of," "rate," and "times" are words that indicate the student should use multiplication. Solving word problems often poses a challenge if terminology comprehension is not reached.

- **Mental math:** Learning how to perform mental math is an asset in solving math problems faster. It's also essential to show children how to use math skills in our everyday lives.
  a. When going out to dinner, have children calculate the tip.
  b. When baking a cake, double the recipe. Children will learn fractions and equations without realizing it.
  c. Our local grocery store offers a discount on gas when customers use their reward card. They can calculate savings when purchasing gas. If I need 15 gallons to fill up my tank and I have a 50-cent per gallon discount on 10 gallons, how much money will I save?

Modern math: Be aware that teaching methods have changed over time, so teaching the way parents learned could be confusing, if children return to brick-and-mortar schools.

MULTIPLICATION:

The problem on the left below illustrates how most people learned multiplication: Multiply 4x6, then 4x3. Next, multiply 2x6, and 2x3. Finally, add the results.

The problem on the right shows how students learn multiplication using the common core standards method. This method is overly complicated for elementary school students.

```
            36                           36
          x 24                         x 24
          ---                          ---
           144  (4 x 36 = 144)          600  (20 x 30 = 600)
         + 720  (2 x 36 = 72            120  (20 x 6 = 120)
          ---   with, 0 added in        120  (4 x 30 = 120)
           864  the ones' position)    + 24  (4 x 6 = 24)
                                       ---
                                        864
```

DIVISION:

The way I learned division in Brazil is different from the way it is taught in the United States.

If the plan is to homeschool through middle school, teach either one of these methods for division. However, if children get transferred back to school and have to show their work, the educator may not be familiar with the Latin American method.

```
    24
3)74
   14
    2
```
United States

```
74 | 3
14   24
 2
```
Latin American countries

DEALING WITH CHILDREN WHO STRUGGLE WITH MATH

Parents often say that they are not good in math, not realizing they pass this mindset on to their children. This attitude deters students from trying to succeed in math and grants them permission to follow suit. To a degree, math ability is genetic; yet, inborn talent is not as critical as determination and hard work. What could be more rewarding than working on a difficult concept and succeeding at it? This is a crucial lesson to learn; generally speaking, once students conquer and succeed in math, nothing in life will seem difficult.

Cultivate a mindset that learning is directly related to the effort put into it. Your job as parents is to be positive role models; help your children understand that math is not beyond their reach and they can be successful if they try. When my husband and I were young, our parents did not help us with homework because that was not the expectation back then. Today, parents are expected to assist children with assignments or hire tutors if they cannot help. Avoid labels and focus on individual effort, which is guaranteed to result in a much-improved outcome.

Psychologist Carol Dweck found that students perform better when they believe they are intelligent and they have much better results when they believe in themselves. "You can always greatly change how intelligent you are," and not have a great outcome if you think "you have a certain amount of intelligence, and you really can't do much to change it." She also believes that when students have a positive attitude, they push themselves harder when others would desist. She believes that there is no limit on their learning potential and challenge is viewed as a way to improve themselves." "They know that their intelligence can be built through experience and effort and are not held back by the idea of inborn restrictions."

I always taught my children that if a concept was difficult to understand, they should simply work harder. If the level on a video game is not challenging, children will not enjoy playing it. Real life problems should not be different.

Math is not beyond anyone's reach if additional effort is put into it.

CHAPTER TEN

OUR CURRICULUM CHOICES FOR WRITING

EVERY SINGLE DAY PEOPLE PUT THE skill of writing to ample use. Homeschool parents often ignore writing until children are in middle school. Learning how to write compositions should start around third grade, allowing students the chance to master the skill by middle school. For most students, writing seems like a difficult feat; however, with the right strategies and tools, any student can succeed. Although most homeschool writing curriculums specify recommended age for each level, I found that most of them do not match the level of writing of public-school students of the same age. Writing is a challenging subject to teach because judging a student's writing is extremely subjective. The way quality of writing is measured at the schools is poorly implemented. A rubric, which is a guideline to score essays, is used in public and most private schools to evaluate organization, development, sentence structure, word choices, grammar usage, and mechanics; however, I found that teachers were notably subjective when grading compositions.

Below is an example of the rubric used for third to fourth graders and the four elements considered by Florida's school system.

- **Focus:** It measures if the main idea is clear and how the context is focused on the topic.
- **Support:** Refers to the details used and development of supporting ideas. The essay must reveal a sense of totality.
- **Organization:** By third grade, students must have logical organization pattern and the composition must have beginning, middle, and conclusion.

- **Convention:** Refers to capitalization, spelling, and sentence structure. In public schools, third and fourth graders are expected to demonstrate a mature command of the language to earn a six out of six score on this level of achievement. They are expected to use subject/verb agreement, complete sentences, and various sentence structures. A one out of six score is given to students who use incorrect spelling, capitalization, punctuation, clichés, or immature word choice. Yes, a third grader should not use immature words. Funny, right?

When my older son was in third grade, he learned about narrative and expository writing. The level of writing expected at such a young age seemed to be extreme, unnecessary, and stressful. Teachers used a rubric to grade the four major areas mentioned above, which is meant to provide a way to be objective.

Third graders were graded on grammatical rules they hadn't even learned yet. My son's compositions had red marks on every line. During a parent-teacher conference, I mentioned to the teacher how difficult it was for my son to see beyond red marks on his composition, e.g., capitalization, punctuation, sentence fragment, sentence structure, subject verb agreement, and transitions. I added that it was difficult for him to be "creative" when he had to concentrate on grammar and spelling.

My son was frustrated and felt that writing was his weakness. The teacher missed my point and instead of correcting the paper with a red pen, she changed it to a blue marker. Obviously, the color of the pen was not the point I was trying to make.

How did we deal with the writing flaws from the public school when we started homeschooling?

We purchased a few writing programs that were too basic and steps too granular, making it difficult for my sons to grasp the big picture. I used a portion of the curriculum listed below for the first few years and eventually came up with my own method to take my children's writing skills to a higher level. This is not meant to be a step-by-step of how to teach writing; it is simply an explanation of the method I used with my sons.

As mentioned earlier, concentrate on the writing portion of the composition. Develop lesson plans based on spelling and grammar errors from their compositions; however, students should be aware that the grade only reflects the writing portion of the composition and other issues will be covered at a later date.

Consider their age, since they acquire more verbal skills as they get older. Search the Internet for explicit rules to aid with grammar and verbal inaccuracies. Whether children need remedial support on a specific subject or more in-depth material to ignite their love for learning, facilitating at home is the solution. The reason I stepped in and worked with my sons when they were in elementary school was primarily because they were not being challenged sufficiently and I wanted to guarantee that they were not discouraged with school. In addition, I did not feel that correcting students on grammar rules they hadn't been exposed to was appropriate.

Writing Strands

Writing Strands level three was the first curriculum we purchased. It covers sentence structure, how to add extra information to a specific subject, and explains the difference between main and supporting ideas. This curriculum proved to be too basic for my 10-year-old and 12-year-old sons, although it was recommended for ages eight to 12.

Level four was designed for 13 to 14-year-olds; however, it was also too basic for my sons. We were, however, able to use a few of the lessons from these books to improve my 10-year-old son's writing weaknesses.

- Adding details to the composition: Lesson one elaborated on the process of adding additional information to different topics. It is essential to use descriptive language and sensory details to paint a picture in readers' minds, making them feel as if they were there. If the subject happened to be Thanksgiving dinner, this lesson explains how to expand on the topic by saying what happened after Thanksgiving dinner, how to illustrate the piled dishes, the process of clearing the table, or how the dishes broke after the person's shirt got caught on the edge of the table.
- The author goes over introduction, body, and conclusion of a composition in a simplistic way.
- Lesson seven of this curriculum provides strategies on how to elaborate on a specific subject, e.g. adding size, color, material, and placement when describing a piece of furniture.

This is a remarkable curriculum for a younger child who has never been introduced to writing or struggles with fundamental writing skills. *Writing Strands* can be used as a learning tool to teach students how to organize their thoughts and transfer them to paper. Their upgraded curriculum offers levels from beginning I through advanced II for students from fifth to ninth grade. Their new curriculum appears to cater to more advanced writers. A placement test is also available online.

Institute for Excellence in Writing (IEW)

If your children feel overwhelmed when asked to write a composition and do not know where to start, this is a good curriculum to use. The incremental step approach is a good starting point. It focuses on basic structure, where students have to come up with key words to convey the main idea.

IEW offers numerous options and the company's interactive website guides parents to the best choice available for each child's writing skill and grade level. The core curriculum was a little pricy, so I decided to participate in one of Andrew Padewa's 10-hour seminars to learn how to apply their writing methods. (Mr. Padewa is IEW's Founder and Director.) I also purchased their theme-based writing lessons. The Medieval History writing lessons are based on major historical figures, e.g., Byzantine Empire, the Battle of Hastings, and other topics. There are 29 lessons that cover writing from key words, summarizing, research, essays, narrative writing, critique, and creative writing. By purchasing the book, students are entitled to download the "Student Resource Notebook." This notebook was a great tool and an excellent addition to assist my sons with writing. It teaches students how to include strong verbs, "ly" adverbs, quality adjectives, five senses and emotions, and transitional words to their composition.

IEW focuses on equipping students with source material. The key word outline method, where students choose three to four key words from each sentence, is used throughout the curriculum. They write sentences based on chosen words. Although this is an acceptable method for a beginner writer who has difficulty putting words on paper, it leaves no room for creativity. If your children can write their own story, skip to the end of the curriculum. One of the disadvantages of this program is that it requires an extensive amount of teacher interaction.

Regardless of which curriculum is chosen, make sure not to overwhelm students with grammar rules when correcting compositions. IEW (a grammar fix-it tool) provides a grading sheet that makes it easier for parents to grade essays. The grading sheet is a great way for parents to keep track of which techniques the student uses. Obviously, only teach a few techniques at a time. Ask children to read the composition out loud to a sibling or other family member. They inevitably will find sentences that do not make sense and make corrections before turning in the paper.

Break writing down into two parts:

Content: Use the composition checklist from the Student Resource Notebook to comment on content only. This helps ensure that the student has a dramatic opening and closing statement, three paragraphs for the body, and a strong conclusion with a final sentence that reflects the title. Once students are comfortable writing and demonstrate that putting ideas on paper is no longer a challenge, start giving feedback on grammar.

- Grammar: Take notes on misspelled works or grammar mistakes and incorporate those errors into a lesson plan for the following week. The following checklist from IEW helps remind students to add stylistic techniques to their compositions.
- Dress-ups
- Stronger verbs
  Instead of "said" use exclaimed, remarked, screamed, or mumbled. Instead of "thought" use believed, imagined, hoped, considered.
- "ly" adverbs: generously, gently, intensely, certainly.
  Choosing adverbs from the list forces students to look up unfamiliar words, improving vocabulary. Watch as their enthusiasm for language acquisition grows with every lesson. The same can be said for strong verbs. Eventually, I removed the "ly" from the grading checklist to avoid bad writing habits, since professional writers view the use of "ly" adverbs as "weak" writing.

> *Excellence in Writing has provided a wonderful writing experience for my kids! Just recently, my 16 year old applied for a reporter job at a local newspaper and has four weeks in a row of being published on the front page!*
>
> **J.P. (Chicago)**

- Quality adjectives
  Instead of "good" use awesome, marvelous, fantastic, or superb. Instead of "like" use crave, enjoy, treasure, or love.
- "ing" words: rushing, providing, rejoicing, suffering, or avoiding.
- Who/which clause that helps describe someone or something.
- Because: Children tend to write short sentences. The use of "because" aids them in combining two sentences from the key-word outline. Eventually, we also removed "because" from our compositions.
- Adverbial clause should be used in the middle of the sentence (when, while, where, since, if, although, or as).

The curriculum slowly adds stylistic styles to every lesson, so students do not get overwhelmed. Prepositions are added later.

"Dress-ups", sentence openers, and decoration styles are stylistic techniques that can be used to improve writing skills.

Advanced techniques used by IEW:

- Banned words: Avoid words that are overused (a lot, fun, really, and get).
- Sentence openers: Use noun or pronoun, preposition (at, down) clausal openers (when, since, where), or "ed" opener (assured, deceived).
- Decorations: Start a sentence with something that makes readers think. For example, "What will the future embrace?"
  Dramatic decoration: "Killer bees attacked."
- Simile or metaphor: A simile compares two things using "as" or "like," while a metaphor is an implied comparison (Zeus is a Greek god.)
- Alliteration: Repeats an opening consonant sound ("For the sky and the sea, and the sea and the sky" from "Rime of the Ancient Mariner" by Samuel Coleridge.)
- Personification: When a lifeless object is gifted with human qualities. (The sun smiled at everyone.)
- Onomatopoeia: Words that suggest exactly what they mean (boom, bang, or clang).

- Transitional words: In addition, repeatedly, and for instance are some examples.

A link with a list of all stylistic techniques is on my website FromHomeschoolToHarvard.com.

If immature vocabulary is used, create a future lesson plan to address this problem. Play games or use Quizlet to learn synonyms and meanings of new words.

What is Quizlet? This free online tool allows students to learn vocabulary through games and create their own sets of flashcards for any subject. While an online database with over 13 million user-created flashcard sets is available, making your own cards guarantees accuracy and empowers students to take responsibility for their vocabulary. Homeschool parents can create a quick multiple-choice quiz using the Quizlet website.

Advanced writers

By the end of sixth grade, my children had mastered the concepts mentioned above. Our next goal was to boost their writing skills to a higher level. The checklist approach, used by IEW, was interesting for a year, but it circumvents creativity. By now my sons were writing basic compositions complete with an introduction, body, and conclusion. They were able to organize their thoughts, present a logical progression of ideas, and support main thoughts.

Below I describe how I introduced my sons to the more analytical and critical-thinking techniques used by universities. This method augments a student's skills and creates a solid writing foundation. It may seem too advanced for middle school students; however, if instructions are followed, students will learn to write at a higher level. The goal was to introduce them to college-level writing –– not necessarily concentrate on sophisticated argumentative and rhetorical strategies expected from college students. I introduced this method to my sons when they were in sixth grade.

Let's review the steps used to write an outline for an analytical, persuasive, or interpretive essay.

Outline

An outline helps organize ideas and arguments. Students can decide on method of presentation and order of importance. Do they have enough proof to back up their inference? If they come up with only one proof under a specific category, perhaps that category needs to be revised. A sentence or topic outline organizes a writer's thoughts. Topic outlines use one or more words to express a main idea that is to be developed in the body of the composition. Sentence outlines use full sentences to formulate and organize ideas.

The outline will include title, introduction, body, and conclusion.

Writing the Introduction:

An introductory paragraph should include the general subject, followed by the narrowed subject, then specific subject, and thesis. This is where students tell readers what the paper is about and what they are trying to prove (the thesis).

Work on the introduction for as long as it takes (it might take a few months), until they master the concept. Let's say, for example, that the topic is "your home town or city." Teach the process of narrowing, or limiting, the topic. Areas of a town could include residential, commercial, educational, recreational, or industrial. Perhaps the student chooses commercial; this is still is a broad subject, so narrow it down to a shopping center or office buildings. If the student opts for a shopping center, pick the specific type, e.g., planned malls. Now we have general, narrowed, and specific subjects. Once they understand the concept, they can write the introduction on a few topics. Do not add the thesis statement yet. Take baby steps and build on them. Once the topic is narrowed, students should think of an attention-grabbing sentence that piques the reader's interest.

Adding the Thesis Statement:

The first part of the thesis statement is the limited subject, which is the mall. The second part is the major inference, which is a generalization or an opinion about the subject. Minor inferences are subtopics within your major inference. They need to be backed up with proof in the form of facts, examples from your source, statistics, or supporting ideas.

Work on these two concepts for a few months before teaching the body and conclusion portion of the composition. Offer constructive feedback in a clear and effective way before discussing items that need improvement. Follow up with examples of how to improve, without discouraging students. Once necessary improvements are reviewed, allow them to rewrite it. Remember to not concentrate on grammatical errors at this point.

The Body of the Composition:

The body should have three main ideas, or arguments, and three proofs to support them. Assist students with the first paragraph, allowing them to develop the idea and present facts and examples to support the argument. Ignore sentences that are not perfect and use this information to develop future lesson plans. It is vital to break the task down into small steps; otherwise it is overwhelming.

Thus far, the composition has an introduction and the first idea in the body of the essay. Spend as much time as needed to perfect each step before moving on to the next idea. Work on each argument until it's as good as it can be before moving on to the conclusion. Brainstorm at least 10 topics and allow students to work on half of them.

Conclusion:

The conclusion reaffirms the thesis, and an insightful sentence should be added to the end of the essay. There are no set formulas for the closing; however, try to summarize the discussion, be concise, memorable, and deliver a firm opinion on the subject. In summary, the conclusion restates the thesis and the main points of the essay, offers a final example to pull it all together, and ends with an insightful remark. We adhered to this method for one school year. By eighth grade, my sons knew how to write a composition using a prompt.

What is a prompt?

A prompt is a statement about a topic or a problem followed by a question that tests a student's analytical skill and ability to deal with controversial issues. Prompts are normally used in college entrance exams and English high school classes.

An essay is a type of composition that describes and analyzes a topic or problem. There are four major types of essay prompts: descriptive, expository, persuasive, and narrative. Prompts don't always specify the form of writing required, and deciphering which one to use can be difficult. There are key words that provide hints as to which type of essay is expected:

Expository: An expository essay prompt has words such as explain, describe, analyze, or compare/contrast. It presents facts and is informative.

Narrative: Key words for narrative essays are tell, describe, or write a story. A narrative essay tells a story about an event and how it unfolds.

Persuasive: Key words can be "why," "argue," or "convince." This type of essay expects authors to take a stand and convince readers to accept the writer's point of view or recommendation.

Descriptive: A descriptive essay describes a person, an object, or an event.

It is important to expose students to different types of compositions. In addition to the essays mentioned above, my sons were exposed to scientific research papers, short and long stories, and music compositions. *Barron's SAT Writing Workbook* provides detailed essay writing instructions with graded sample essays that expand on ideas for different topics.

Since no single writing curriculum is academically rigorous, a combination of the types mentioned above along with an introduction to college writing helps guarantee good results. Focus on an incremental approach to teach writing skills.

WRITING A NOVEL

Writing a novel ignites children's imaginations. They learn how to set the plot, develop characters, and create scenes. It builds vocabulary, improves communication skills, and even helps release stress.

I purchased the book *Learn to Write the Novel Way*. This book presents a step-by-step writing process that engages students in the task of writing, editing, and publishing their first novel. It also teaches vocabulary, grammar, and composition skills. The book is intended for fifth to 12th grade students; yet, I recommend it for middle school only.

By breaking the process into bite-sized steps, it shows students how to create a plot, organize thoughts, introduce the protagonist, the villain, and finally how to write a novel. I incorporated these concepts into my language arts and writing curriculum; luckily, my sons continued to write their novels on their free time for pleasure.

Both of my sons started countless short and long stories. Yet, they did not follow through with the majority of them. If they decided that the story did not turn out the way they envisioned, they were allowed to stop writing it. Although I prefer that my children finish what they start, I feel writing a novel is an exception. My sons appreciated the freedom of starting new thrillers whenever they pleased. One of them wrote a 300-page science fiction novel during our vacation to North Carolina. He was 13.

During our cross-country trip to 17 states and Canada, we asked our boys to write about every state we visited. Besides historical facts, they wrote about our camping experiences and sites visited. *Illustory Make-A-Book* is a complete kit that can be used for writing and illustrating a storybook, poems, or a picture book. Children write a story, upload it to the Illustory website and receive a hardcover book by mail. It was fascinating to read both books and note that even though they visited the same sites, the information in each book was completely different.

The website is also valuable for those children who are interested in self-publishing their own drawings, poems, or stories. The book even comes with an About-the-Author page, and pictures and drawings can be added to it.

Our results using the writing method above

When my son was 15, he was taking ENC1101 college composition. He scored 100 percent on every composition he wrote. The professor was so impressed with his writing skill, that she entered his paper in the university's writing contest without his knowledge. All the students who took ENC 1101 and ENC 1102 were eligible to participate. I'm proud to say that even though he was competing against much older college students, who were mostly English majors, he won first place.

CURSIVE WRITING

Unlike the United States, other countries teach cursive writing when students are in the first grade. All the elementary school books are written in cursive; therefore, children are expected to learn it. Due to the technological changes, the need to learn cursive writing has diminished; however, there will always be situations where children need to read in cursive. For example, they may receive

handwritten notes from teachers, co-workers, or family members. Although it will not impact their chances of entering college or getting a job, cursive writing is destined to be in their lives for at least another 50 years before it becomes obsolete. Since my sons were taught how to read and write in Portuguese and cursive writing was a requirement, they were able to read letters sent from my mom.

What a delight to observe my sons as they read letters written in this beautiful, soon-to-be-lost art form. They used cursive practice worksheets for five minutes a day to improve their writing. Not an enormous effort for such a rewarding result.

CHAPTER ELEVEN

OUR CURRICULUM CHOICES FOR LANGUAGE ARTS

LEARNING HOW TO READ

SURPRISINGLY ENOUGH, CHILDREN TODAY ARE expected to know how to read by the time they enter kindergarten. When my first son started kindergarten, he did not know how to read or write. He was already learning two languages, so I felt that teaching him how to read at age three was unnecessary.

I was astonished to hear from his teacher that he was "behind." She had more "advanced" students who already knew how to read. This was before the mandatory Pre-K we have today. How disappointing to know that parents had to be responsible to teach their children at such a young age. Luckily, he learned fast and was at the same level as all the other students in no time at all.

I had taken a leave of absence from my job at Motorola, so I had the opportunity to go back to college and take educational classes. My younger son was home with me and although I strongly disagreed, I felt pressured to teach him how to write and read before age four. I wanted to make sure that he did not fall behind when he entered kindergarten. (I know, that is absurd!)

I came across the website *Zac the Rat* from Starfall Education (Starfall.com), which helps children in a dynamic and interactive manner. These phonic lessons benefit visual and auditory learners using silly sounds. *Zac the Rat* makes learning fun for students as high as second grade. When students click on a letter of the alphabet, the software provides activities intended to help them recall each letter associated with each sound. It teaches students how to read, focusing on how the sounds of the letters fit into short sentences. Animations are used throughout the program, with activities where students learn how to read sentences in a fun and entertaining way. The final step is to learn how to read by using phonics. This section provides children with fiction and non-fiction books to practice their reading skills. I also used a phonics reading program I had at home; however, my children would much rather interact with *Zac the Rat*.

READING WITH CHILDREN

Reading to younger children significantly expands their reading and writing skills and improves concentration, vocabulary and listening skills, stimulates imagination, and teaches appreciation for literature that is too advanced for young children to read on their own. Every parent spends hours every night reading or telling stories to their children when they are young. This bonding time with children is invaluable; however, as children mature, they no longer have the desire to be read to. Parents have difficulty with that transition; yet, it is a stress-free adjustment for children.

We stopped reading children's storybooks when my sons were 10 to 11 years old and no longer found bedtime stories interesting. By middle school, we read novels based on history rather than storybooks. *My Name Is America* novels are based on stories that happened during historical events (World War II, Battle of Fredericksburg or Plymouth) told through the eyes of teenagers.

I tried to still be involved in their reading assignments by using SparkNotes, which offers readers a chapter-by-chapter summary of novels and metaphorical meanings of words or phrases. This tool should only be used after students finish reading the novel. *Lord of the Flies* is an interesting book that provides an in-depth understanding of figurative meanings, because symbolism plays a significant role in the story. Each object and character has significance. For example, Piggy's glasses represent intelligence, and the island with the water current flowing in reverse symbolizes the world and implies that the civilization is regressing.

> *We love to read stories with historical facts. I know my kids remember more (especially my auditory learner). They get more of a feeling of what it was like back in those days. It is easier to have discussions and learn from other people's mistakes or successes.*
>
> **E. P. (New York)**

SparkNotes include everything noteworthy that happens in a chapter as well as an analysis of main characters. Along with your children, use this tool a few times to analyze different stories; eventually they will automatically recognize and utilize this process. They also learn to read slower and grasp the hidden meanings in symbolic writing.

Document funny comments your children make, so you can remember these comical conversations. One of our family's funniest stories was when we went to the beach and my son noticed that my husband had chest hair and I didn't, so he said "Mom, don't be sad. When you get older you will get hair on your chest, too." Read the stories during family gatherings. Our tradition is to read them around our annual New Year's bonfire in North Carolina.

My younger child, who was an avid reader, had difficulty writing compositions. In contrast, my elder son, who did not like reading for fun, was a great writer. Although studies claim that there is a relationship between reading and writing, there is little practical evidence of that in this relationship.

ENGLISH

The best predictors of a student's academic success are comprehension and writing skills. I selected a curriculum that uses literature as a foundation and focused on teaching thinking and communication skills, using literature as a base.

English was covered four times a week for 45 minutes each day. I assigned 20 new vocabulary words every Monday and my boys spent 15 minutes each day studying them, using Quizlet. They took a test, generated by the software, every Friday.

We purchased *Learning Language Arts Through Literature*. In addition, I designed grammar lessons based on mistakes found in their compositions. *Learning Language Arts Through Literature* lays the groundwork for reading, writing, vocabulary, and comprehension. It uses literature as a foundation, which was an important part of keeping this subject interesting for my avid-reader child. It follows Charlotte Mason's approach, which concentrates on short lessons, narration, and dictation. Lessons include copying literature passages, spelling words from the passage, and writing the passage from dictation; it also covers basic language analogies, parts of speech, and punctuation. Writing assignments include narrative, descriptive, and how-to essay topics throughout the year. Vocabulary words should come from all the different subjects learned at that grade level.

Grade six lessons require students to read and analyze novels, such as Carry on, Mr. Bowditch. The 36 weekly lessons include grammar, dictation, spelling, and writing. *Learning Language Arts Through Literature* for grade seven requires students to analyze plays, such as Shakespeare's *Much Ado About Nothing* and covers poetry, novel analysis, short stories, and research units. This book is ideal for children who can work independently.

SPEED-READING

There is no doubt that speed-reading increases performance and many companies offer speed-reading courses to help employees in an effort to double productivity.

It is beneficial to increase reading speed as long as it does not affect comprehension. Choosing programs that improve reading speed along with comprehension and information retention is key to success.

If someone is reading for pleasure, speed-reading is not a concern. However, slow readers may not be able to finish a test or homework on time, affecting their grade. Interactive speed-reading software can help students read faster; however, the ones with an intuitive interface and preliminary speed assessment linked to comprehension are the best.

Although my son had straight A's while in elementary school, his teacher felt that his reading speed was slow compared to other students. She tried to help by having him read the same passage day after day. Obviously, if a student reads the same passage over and over again, he would read that passage faster. Second, what is the point of reading fast if it impairs comprehension?

We purchased *The Reader's Edge*, which teaches speed-reading using an interactive CD program. When students first start using the program, it tests their reading speed and uses that as a baseline.

The advantage of this program is that improving reading speed by two to five times does not affect reading comprehension. The program works by decreasing eye fixations and teaches students to read a group of letters, instead of a single word at a time.

By specifying reading goals, which can be set by each student, the program helps increase reading speed. My elder son used this program for six months and quadrupled his reading speed. My younger son's reading speed was too fast already, so we used the program to improve comprehension.

WHY IS READING COMPREHENSION IMPORTANT?

Reading comprehension is the ability to process information and understand the content read. Since reading is the foundation for all academic subjects, reading fluency is vital to succeed in school. If students don't understand what they are reading, they fall behind, which consequently affects their overall academic success. Comprehension is an essential skill if children want to ace standardized tests. My son struggled with reading and comprehension strategies such as making predictions, drawing conclusions, making inferences, and identifying author's purpose. He was only 8 years old when he said, "Mom, the teacher expects me to know why the author wrote this article, but I have never met him…so I can't ask." I needed material that had plenty of examples, allowing him to practice the skill repeatedly. I purchased STARS®, which focuses on 12 key reading strategies:

1. Understanding sequence: Sequencing skill allows students to retell the story in sequence and not just focus on the parts that were most appealing to them.

2. Recognizing cause and effect: Recognizing that an event is responsible for the cause that leads to the effect. This skill generates analytical thinkers. According to Piaget's theory, a child cannot think logically until the concrete operational stage (7 to 11-years-old). So, when public school teachers expect second grade students to be at this stage, they are pushing the envelope and end up frustrating them because they progress at different rates.

3. Finding the main idea: The main idea is usually found in the first sentence of the story, and is the most important idea in the paragraph. The ability to find and identify the main idea is important not only when taking English classes, but also to extract information from textbooks for other subjects. A bullet outline is an effective way to help students understand what they read.

4. Comparing and contrasting: Students learn to compare how two or more items or passages are similar or dissimilar.

5. Finding word meaning in context: Students learn how to use the other words in a sentence or passage to understand an unknown word.

6. Drawing conclusions and making inferences: Understanding when information is implied.

7. Distinguishing fact from opinion: While facts can be proved, opinions cannot. Opinions usually come after words such as believe, feel, or think.

8. Making predictions: Students use their own personal experience to foresee what they are about to read.

9. Identifying author's purpose: Authors can persuade readers to believe in something or inform them about a topic.

10. Summarizing: Students learn how to describe what they read in their own words, ignore irrelevant information, and discern which ideas are important.

11. Recalling facts and details: Understanding how to differentiate passages that contain facts and details helps a student's understanding of the story and main idea.
12. Interpreting figurative language: Students understand how to differentiate a simile, metaphor, or idiom. This skill becomes more important in middle or high school.

These strategies improve comprehension, which is a higher-level skill that should be reinforced year after year. Research shows that there is correlation between mastering this skill and academic success.

CHAPTER TWELVE

OUR CURRICULUM CHOICES FOR SCIENCE

LEARNING SCIENCE CAN BE EXCITING, as long as teachers have theoretical and practical knowledge to convey information in a fun and informative way. A number of professions require a strong math and science background. Using the right tools to teach these subjects allows children to acquire the knowledge required to pursue any career they desire in the future.

It is essential to gauge a student's prior knowledge to define what to teach. Supplement your curriculum with interactive and hands-on activities that use inexpensive everyday items. Games, videos, magazines, field trips, and science experiments can be engaging and fun. Children can gain vast amounts of knowledge from the Internet or TV, without even realizing these shows are being used as educational tools.

Science was on our schedule four times a week for an hour. Since my sons were two years apart, there were topics that my elder son had already studied; as a result, science topics were chosen for each one individually. Although I enjoyed teaching and performing experiments with them, we also had lessons they could complete on their own.

BrainPOP

When my children were younger, *BrainPOP* was a popular website. This online software creates animated and curriculum-based content that engages students in learning science and other subjects in a fun and interactive way. This is a wonderful way to review complex subject matter that is easily searchable with an online tool. Avraham Kadar, M.D., an immunologist and pediatrician, created *BrainPOP* to explain difficult concepts to his young patients. This is a great tool to review or introduce topics in a general sense; however, I don't recommend it for exploring a subject or topic in-depth. The videos can also be used for remediation purposes.

Apologia

Exploring Creation With General Science (seventh grade) and *Exploring Creation With Physical Science* (eighth grade) are Christian-based curriculums, and the author does not hide his bias toward a young-earth position. Only teach those chapters that benefit your children and supplement with other books, field trips, or video streaming from Discovery Channel and other educational shows.

Scientifically savvy parents can use the first chapter of this book as a valuable launching pad to discuss age-of-the-earth controversy with their children. The author lays out both young-earth and old-earth creation positions. This curriculum could be a source of misperception for students since the topic on uniformitarian and its approach to geology diverges from the position endorsed by the majority of geologists.

The Physical Science book casts doubts on the reliability of radiometric dating methods, which could be a source of confusion for students. A parent's job is to show both sides and then have a discussion with their children. Another solution is to skip those controversial topics until children are mature enough to understand them.

I selected chapters that I wanted to cover with my children, skipping topics that would not benefit them. The General Science book starts the chapter with lengthy discussions on the history of science. I felt my middle-school-aged children would not find this information interesting enough to warrant page after page of tedious explanation.

Using this curriculum as one of the sources to teach science is a valuable addition. The in-depth explanations on every topic allow students to correlate the material learned with the science experiments performed after each topic. The author's conversational approach is more interesting than traditional science textbooks and helps parents teach the subject even without previous scientific background.

These two books are the primary curriculums we used, and on those days I found myself too busy with my second child or had household issues to resolve, allowed my older son to work on his own using Exploration Education curriculum. We performed all the experiments together, and I was impressed with the experiments and the step-by-step explanations on the results.

Exploration Education

Exploration Education is an interactive science curriculum. The physical science intermediate level was designed for fourth to sixth grade. The series also offers advanced physical science for seventh through 10th grade.

The hands-on activities, which were part of the intermediate physical science curriculum, were my son's favorite and an ideal curriculum for fourth or fifth grade. However, there are not enough details to keep a sixth grader engaged. The advanced and intermediate levels cover the same topics in more depth. My son loved building the projects and appreciated the interactive explanations.

One downside was that if students wanted to review a specific topic, the program would send them to the beginning of the lesson and repeat the entire lesson before getting to the desired page. (The software company may have revised the code and corrected this issue by now.)

The projects were interesting and correlated to topics covered in the book. Projects include a weight balance scale, guitar, boat, and solar panel. This is a highly engaging curriculum; however, purchase the advanced kit if your homeschoolers excel in science. Although recommended for grade levels four through 10, my experience shows that it only benefits grades four through six. The advanced curriculum includes all the lessons from the standard kit, plus three extra projects that are more challenging. Force and motion, electricity, and chemistry are some topics covered by this curriculum. Questions after each lesson, with multiple attempts to obtain the correct answer, allow students to review the material. After learning each lesson, students can work on experiments.

Instructions are comprehensive and students can easily complete assignments without assistance. There are two quizzes at the end of each of the eight units, and four exams, each covering two of the units. There is a logbook that can be used to record observations from experiments.

Interactive learning

Children who have the opportunity to employ their senses retain extra information. Their linguistic, social, and creative skills are cultivated when diverse supplies are used and experimental data analyzed. Science infuses a sense of intrigue and curiosity, and when children excel in science, they develop critical-thinking skills. Most of my sons' birthday and Christmas gifts were related to science.

- When in elementary school, we purchased a butterfly garden kit. What an interesting and creative way to study insect metamorphosis — observing painted lady caterpillars as they mature, transform into chrysalises, and finally emerge as butterflies. When they were fully grown, we released them.

- We used hatchery frog kits to study lifecycle frogs. We observed tiny embryos develop into tadpoles that grew legs and developed into frogs.

- Going to the beach and building volcanos on the sand was one of our favorite activities. It demonstrates how chemical reaction can simulate real physical volcano eruption by simply using baking soda, dish detergent, and vinegar.

- The National Wildlife Federation offers programs where children can become "scientists" by recording and observing wildlife and plants in their area. Data is forwarded to scientists, who then track the health and behavior of wildlife and plant species nationwide.

- Slime can be made using food coloring, borax, glue, and water.

- Online science museums add educational value to any curriculum.

- Learn about human and animal anatomy by purchasing anatomical models that provide details of human or animal body parts.

- *InnerBody* website offers an interactive tool for middle and high school students to learn about human anatomy. This comprehensive guide allows students to study 13 major anatomic systems. Besides an explanation on each body system, the tool uses 3D illustrations where students explore the human body.
- A thermometer can be used to track weather. Students can use the data to create a line, bar, pie, histogram, or scatter graph with the results.

Static electricity, light and color, bottle rocket, and soil erosion are topics that can be explored. These and other similar activities allowed us to spend time as a family, learn different concepts, and understand our surroundings.

The importance of performing science experiments using sensory play

Gathering material and making time to carry out science experiments can be time consuming, nevertheless rewarding when we understand the benefits in engaging our children in these activities. Science experiments refine social, physical, creative, cognitive, and linguistic skills. Sensory information goes to the thalamus (gray matter of the brain) when we hear, see, or taste something. This is the area of the brain that assists in processing information and sends this data to other parts of the brain. The information is afterwards sent to the hippocampus, which is responsible for memory. The amygdala handles the emotional and memory processing.

Certain smells bring us back to a specific location and time, allowing us to remember an event that, in turn, influences our mood. Smell can trigger detailed memory or emotion because our olfactory bulb is directly connected to the hippocampus and amygdala, bypassing the thalamus and going straight to the brain's smell center. A familiar odor binds to the nose's receptor and this smell can trigger a memory of a special event, place, holiday, or childhood experience.

Cognitive skills allow children to gain understanding from experiences and enable them to process new information. New skills help students comprehend the world around them and think at higher levels, process information, and make connections to other events effortlessly. Without realizing it, children grow into little scientists and develop analytical skills by making observations and predictions.

Homeschoolers have time to explore, perform experiments, and learn new concepts. Since collecting material for science experiments is time consuming, gather them ahead of time. Ready-made kits can be expensive; nonetheless, they can save time. Many experiments can be performed with household items. For example, you can construct an electric motor with copper wire, clay, batteries, a piece of wood, knife, cork, pins, and knitting needle.

Perform experiments that involve all students

If siblings work together, they have the opportunity to learn from each other. Children also learn by sharing their ideas with others. If one of the children is too young to understand the experiment, have material available to explore hand-eye coordination –– tie shoes or zip zippers to develop fine motor skill or throw a ball to develop gross motor skills. Assuming the chemical used is not harmful, younger children can help mix, measure, or pour required materials for the experiment.

Even though the little ones are not learning all the details of the experiment, they learn to think creatively and build problem-solving skills.

How to entertain young children:

- Paint each other's faces.
- Tie-dye T-shirts.
- Play or listen to an instrument.
- Play educational games.
- Add food coloring to bath water.
- Try to guess sounds heard outside.
- Play musical chairs.
- Let them paint the inside of the dishwasher door. This was one of my sons' favorite activities. After they create their masterpiece, close the door and run the dishwasher. Be sure to take a picture first.
- Adjust music volume up and down to teach them about loud and soft sounds.
- Cook using different scents (garlic, ginger, lemon, vinegar, or mint).

- Compare different foods: frozen versus hot, salty versus sweet, and crunchy versus soft.

Invest in a microscope early on, since it will be used through high school. A cheap microscope often becomes frustrating for students. Check out local school auctions to see if you can find a high-quality microscope at a reasonable price. A pair of binoculars is also an asset when exploring the outdoors. A USB computer microscope is a good option as well.

CHAPTER THIRTEEEN

OUR CURRICULUM CHOICES FOR SOCIAL STUDIES

HISTORY

DIG UP THE PAST AND SHOW STUDENTS how history is an essential part of everyday life. History comes alive by studying our own heritage and visiting historical sites. It should never be dull, nor throw anyone into a loop of endless memorizing of names and dates.

A globe, world maps, and atlas are essential to study history and geography. Blank timeline sheets can be purchased for each period of history. We displayed them in a prominent place for a few months, as we studied those time periods. By placing people and events in chronological order, students do not jumble up concepts and facts, and they are able to put names, places, and events in sequence. It helps them understand the big picture and the implications of current events. As children watch the news, relate what is happening now with what occurred in the past. Old maps are an asset and can be compared with recent versions. Maps of the world have changed numerous times over the years, so take the opportunity to compare these maps and point out differences and historical facts behind the changes.

History Odyssey

My husband volunteered to teach this subject to our children, although he had a full-time job as Director of Engineering and Technology at Motorola/Google. He chose *History Odyssey* as our main curriculum because it gave a chronological and comprehensive study of ancient, middle age, early- modern and modern history. *History Odyssey* teaches history by analyzing different cultures and their influences in different areas of the world. Plus, it encompasses the literature, historical events, and geography of each time period. It emphasizes literary analysis, writing skills, research skills, and timeline analysis.

Although this is not a Christian curriculum, I feel that parents can take this opportunity to reinforce family beliefs and have open discussions with children on different viewpoints. These underlying suppositions can serve as a launch pad for discussion and sharpen children's critical-thinking skills.

The study guide that is part of the *History Odyssey* curriculum uses the *Story of Mankind* by Hendrik Willem van Loon, Kingfisher History Encyclopedia, and other supplemental quality literature as references. In addition, it contains lesson plans, weekly reading lists, daily activities, and focuses on outlining and summarizing learned material.

Other resources

American History comes alive with videos and games.

- Gettysburg DVD, directed by Ronald Maxwell, is based on Michael Shaara's Pulitzer Prize-winning novel *The Killer Angels*. It dramatizes the events that occurred at Gettysburg, Pennsylvania, July 1-3, 1863.
- Time Travelers U.S. History Studies (The American Revolution)
- This series explains the politics and battles behind the birth of a new nation.
- The Civil War series includes 25 lessons, covering politics and conflicts that nearly ripped apart a nation. Additional topics include slavery, emancipation, retreats, battles, leaders, women of the war, and Reconstruction.
- *Story of the World* by Susan Wise, also available on CD, teaches history in chronological order, and is entertaining and

educational. The curriculum is not as comprehensive as that of *History Odyssey*. The CDs are perfect for long road trips.

- *The Civil War* by Ken Burns is a documentary that meticulously traces the War Between the States through the years. It contains some violent scenes, so it is not appropriate for young children.

- The *My Name Is America* novels feature stories told through the eyes of boys from ages 12 to 16. *The Journal of Rufus Rowe* (a story about the Battle of Fredericksburg), *The Journal of Scott Pendleton Collins* (a story of a World War II soldier), and *The Journal of Jasper Jonathan Pierce* (a story of a pilgrim that took place in Plymouth in 1620) describe events that took place during their lifetimes in different parts of the world.

Learning during a cross-country trip

Homeschoolers have the opportunity to travel and learn on the road. Traveling provides life lessons that cannot be taught in school. Whether you travel to another country, state, or within your own city, it is an invaluable learning experience. Children become more tolerant to changes and more confident when it comes to experimenting with new adventures. Involve children in the planning stages: establishing a budget, looking over maps, and choosing activities for the family. Take virtual tours of places on your itinerary and read about their traditions and history.

Our cross-country trip from Florida to Canada was done during the school year to avoid crowds at the national parks. The purpose of this trip was to learn American History and geography by visiting sites where historical events took place. An added bonus: State and municipal parks are ideal for camping.

In less than three months, our family visited 17 states and every civil and revolutionary war site in the area. National park rangers are exceptionally knowledgeable about the history of their region and are able to tell stories as if they had lived in that time period.

Reenactments that restage civil or revolutionary battles are common in national parks throughout the country. The reenactment of the battle of Gettysburg, which included the Union and Confederate's infantry, artillery, and cavalry, made history books come alive.

We also purchased a self-guiding auto tour compact disk to learn more details about the battle at Gettysburg as we drove through the site.

In Philadelphia, we visited the Christ Church Cemetery where Founding Father Benjamin Franklin is buried. What a unique opportunity to teach children the impact that Benjamin Franklin had as a writer, scientist, inventor, abolitionist, civic activist, and diplomat. Research facts associated with these sites prior to visiting them.

In Vermont, we visited Ben & Jerry's flavor graveyard. The granite tombstone has signs of 40 former flavors that are discontinued. Schweddy Balls (vanilla with rum) and Chubby Hubby (vanilla, pretzels, and peanut butter) are some of the flavors that ended up in their boneyard.

State History

Traveling to historical sites in your state and stopping at famous landmarks is an efficient and worthwhile way to learn, so use a textbook only as a reference. Organize a trip to your local City Hall, attend City Council meetings, and visit historical sites.

Castillo de San Marcos in St. Augustine, Ocala Historic District, Harry S. Truman House in Key West, and the Bonnet House in Fort Lauderdale are examples of Florida's historical landmarks we visited.

- St. Augustine is a charming city founded in 1585.
- Ocala Historic District is home to more than 200 beautiful structures in Florida.
- Harry S. Truman Little White House is a State Heritage Landmark. Built in 1890 as naval officers' quarters, it was fitted out with furnishings purchased by the Navy for President Truman. William Taft, Franklin Roosevelt, Dwight Eisenhower, John Kennedy, Jimmy Carter, and Bill Clinton used the site as a retreat.
- The Bonnet House Museum & Gardens: Historic home in Fort Lauderdale listed in the U.S. National Register of Historical Places.

GEOGRAPHY

History Odyssey's curriculum combines history, geography, and writing in its lessons. Geography is interlinked with history and maps, which offers a pronounced understanding of each region of study. Map skill lessons compare ancient and modern cities, and students also learn about locations of rivers, oceans, and countries. Although geography weaves itself into historical studies, incorporating drill work in our curriculum proved to be essential. Memorization has its benefits and should not be overdone; however, there are times when it can benefit students. This skill serves as mental exercise as children learn detailed information about U.S. states, their capitals, or any mundane fact that might benefit them in the future.

Select one country a week to study. Learn to cook ethnic food and use Google Earth to visit all the famous sites. Family heritage history can be incorporated into history, geography, reading, research, and writing.

Ideas for fun activities:

Use a Pocket Chart to Learn New Facts: A pocket chart system can be used to learn new facts about politics, geography, or history. Add new facts to the chart every Monday and spend a few minutes introducing each topic. Ask children to go over the cards every day for about three minutes. Once a month, collect all the cards. The child who remembers the most facts, wins the game.

What to put on the chart:

- State flashcards using mnemonics are helpful when learning states and their capitals. Memory Joggers has a unique way to teach

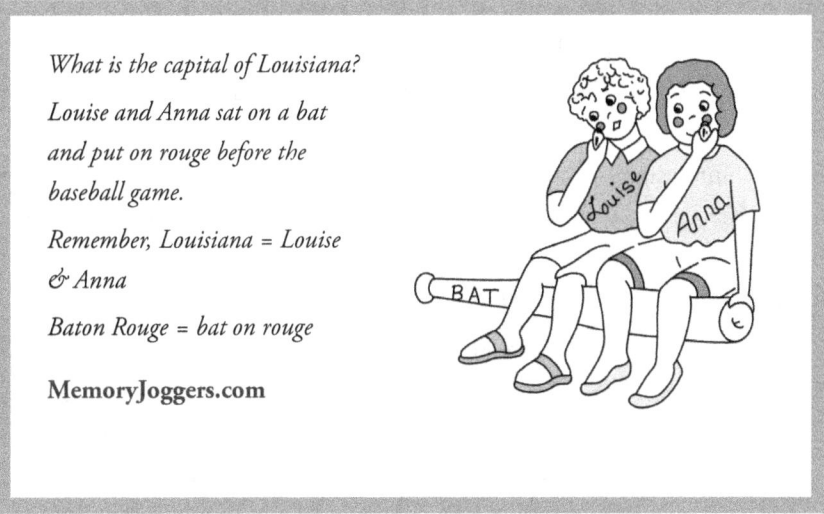

What is the capital of Louisiana?
Louise and Anna sat on a bat and put on rouge before the baseball game.
Remember, Louisiana = Louise & Anna
Baton Rouge = bat on rouge

MemoryJoggers.com

Learn facts about each state, as well. For example, did you know that Alabama workers built the first rocket to put humans on the moon?

- Studying about the countries that are part of the Seven Wonders of the Ancient World and the Seven Wonders of the World can be a fun way to learn about sites with historical value. The Great Pyramid of Giza, built in a time period of 85 years, is one of the Seven Wonders of the Ancient World. Google Earth provides a high-resolution satellite image of famous sites. The ability to swivel the camera perspective to view landscape topography and take a 3D walking tour makes learning enjoyable.
- Learn the names of United States presidents.

Educational Games: Play educational games such as Map Tangle.

The goal of this game is to locate landmarks, countries, rivers, and deserts around the world. Teach some facts beforehand to ensure familiarity with landmarks, making playing the game more interesting. Remove half of the cards they are not familiar with and slowly add them to the pocket chart activity above. (Due to a recall for potential lead poison on this item in 2005, do not buy a used one.)

Spy Games: *Highlights Top Secret* is a game that allows children to participate in adventures and solve mysteries that take place in a specific country. They solve a puzzle to get clues about the crime. Each clue is used as the child learns about each country's geography, history, and culture.

Virtual Tour: After the 2001 terrorist attacks, visiting the White House is no longer an effortless task. An alternative is to relish a panoramic tour of the White House online that allows visitors to view the Blue Room, Cabinet Room, China Room (where the official porcelain dishes of past presidents are kept), Oval Office, Red Room, and Roosevelt Room. My children appreciated the architectural details by zooming in on each object (sculptures, portraits of former presidents, and pottery).

Learning Geography: Geography should not stop in your country of origin. Expand an appreciation for other traditions and cultures. We were fortunate enough to be able to travel to other countries and experience diverse cultures, religions, agriculture, and climate. If travelling is not an option due to cost or time, an alternative is to pick a country per month and study its culture, cuisine, and climate at home by searching on the Internet and in books.

- On a wall map, highlight the country of choice.
- Cook meals that are part of the local cuisine.
- Ask young children to draw the flag for that country.
- Google all the main landmarks and make a list of them.
- Use Google Earth to locate landmarks.
- Learn a few sentences in the country's language.
- Search for local museums that offer virtual tours and explore their history.
- Work on a travel brochure for that country and have a competition among your children. Every month select the winner; before the school year is over, reward the overall winner with a favorite field trip or an outing to a restaurant that serves the local cuisine of one of the countries studied.

Learn About National Holidays: Check for holidays celebrated each month and study the meaning of each event. St. Patrick's Day, Mardi Gras, Kentucky Derby, Cinco de Mayo, Martin Luther King Jr., Day, President's Day, and Labor Day are holidays we celebrate.

Educational TV Channels: History and Discovery channels offer educational shows. *How the States Got Their Shape*s is not only educational, but brings over 500 years of American History to life. The journey goes far beyond geography and explores the history and peculiarities of each state, including each state's population and how each state was divided.

Educational Computer Games: My sons loved SimCity™ software, which they played in their free time. They learned about different cultures, ecosystems, energy, ethics, design and planning, health, natural resources, waste, pollution, environmental footprint, agriculture, consumption, climate change, the water and watershed of a city. The game allows players to build a metropolis, while maintaining the happiness and health of its citizens. They figure out how to expand their city and stay within budget while developing the industrial, residential, and commercial areas. As the city grows, players have to worry and resolve issues related to education and health.

In order to avoid a workers' strike, players must provide sufficient funding for services. Parks, roads, subways, stadiums, airports, bus stops, and seaports have to be added to the city. Players can choose sustainable energy options for the city, such as wind farms, geothermal, and solar. Every choice made affects the city and the world within the game.

What a tremendous opportunity to teach children the importance of making the right decisions for the environment. Create lesson plans that encourage children to think critically and learn problem-solving skills regarding challenges facing modern cities. Students will learn new skills through urban planning and environmental management.

If the right choice is made, the child earns points. Raising taxes causes the player to lose 10 points.

CIVICS

We the People: The Citizen & the Constitution is a great curriculum that teaches middle and high school students about government and citizenship. This textbook encompasses critical-thinking exercises that enhance a student's understanding of American constitutional democracy. Questions at the end of each chapter engage students in open discussion about constitutional principles and how to become respectable citizens. As students analyze and gain critical-thinking skills, they are expected to analyze historical events, take a position on several topics, and discuss a multitude of issues.

At the beginning of each lesson, a vocabulary list is provided. Use Quizlet to learn new words and create your vocabulary of the week. The software saves all previous vocabulary words, so they can be reviewed at a later date to gauge how well students retain information. In summary, this book provides opportunities for students to read about our government, present their point of view, and practice their writing skills throughout each lesson.

Since 2010, Florida required middle school students to take a semester of civics. Although this subject is optional for homeschoolers, my sons studied civics for a year. Teachers in the public school system tend to emphasize the rudimentary facts of government; however, homeschoolers can concentrate on teaching ideologies that can be applied in everyday life. The benefit of learning at home is that children can become proficient on important topics, such as how to interpret political information, how to discuss political issues with peers or adults, help their community, and discuss topics related to the political system of the United States.

Since my sons were boy scouts and had to work on merit badges related to citizenship, we were able to reinforce what they learned. Citizenship in the community's merit badge booklet discusses the rights and duties of a citizen. On one of the assignments, scouts have to select an issue that is important to the community and discuss it with local government agents.

My sons interviewed local authorities on the importance of protecting leatherback sea turtles, which are endangered. Sea turtle hatchlings use the reflection from the moon to find their way to the ocean. Artificial coastal lighting, such as streetlights, disorients hatchlings and causes them to emerge from their nests and go toward bright lights, instead of the ocean, causing thousands of hatchling deaths each year.

It also discourages sea turtles from laying eggs. The city counts on the assistance of volunteers to educate local businesses on the importance of replacing bright lights with amber colored lights. We volunteered for the Sea Turtle Oversight Protection Organization and, along with guiding turtles towards the ocean when they became disoriented, also distributed pamphlets educating the community on the importance of this ordinance. My sons also participated in the city's code enforcement meetings to understand local issues.

For the Citizenship in the Nation merit badge, they had to visit a National Historic Landmark. We visited the Bonnet House Museum & Gardens, which is an 1895 plantation-style home located in Fort Lauderdale.

Both of my sons volunteered hundreds of hours of community service for nonprofit organizations, such as the Homeless Shelter's Food Drive, Sea Turtle Oversight Protection, Tomorrow's Rainbow, Sawgrass Wildlife Center, Relay for Life, Christmas Toy Drive, AMSA Breast Cancer Drive, and AMSA Alzheimer's Walk.

ADDITIONAL SUBJECTS

Physical Education

Exercise as a family to establish a healthy pattern. Working out helps children sleep better, build strong bones, and self-esteem. Children who are physically active are more likely to be academically successful and motivated. My children participated in organized sports, walked daily, and biked. Although our daily walk was not their favorite activity, they eventually understood the benefits of exercise and started an exercise routine on their own.

They joined the high school soccer, swim, and track varsity teams. Homeschool children can jog, bike, walk, or dance; in addition, yacht clubs offer sailing and tennis classes. Some local public middle and high schools permit homeschoolers to participate in their competitive sports, such as baseball, tennis, soccer, tag football, swimming, and basketball.

Team sports assist in developing cooperation, social skills, and self-assurance. Besides, a coach who is thoughtful and skilled can have a remarkable impact on children's lives. Individual sports help develop perseverance, focus, confidence, and self-reliance. SAINTS is an accredited physical education program where students meet in state parks in Florida, Texas, California, and Nevada. My sons participated in the program once a week from 9 a.m. to 4 p.m. Students were separated into groups, according to their ages. They played soccer, basketball, track and field, golf, tennis, archery, softball, Frisbee, kite flying, t-ball, and flag football.

States that allow homeschoolers to join their public schools' extracurricular activities

Alabama, Alaska, Arkansas, Colorado, Florida, Idaho, Indiana, Iowa, Louisiana, Maine, Maryland, Massachusetts, Minnesota, Missouri, New Hampshire, New Mexico, North Dakota, Ohio, Oregon, Pennsylvania, Rhode Island, South Carolina, South Dakota, Tennessee, Utah, Vermont, Wisconsin, and Wyoming allow homeschoolers to participate in public school interscholastic extracurricular activities.

- Part-time enrollment is permitted in Illinois; however, homeschoolers can rarely join their sports teams.
- Homeschoolers can participate in extracurricular activities in Montana, New York, and Oklahoma if they are enrolled at the school full time.
- Michigan and Nebraska permit homeschoolers to participate in public school extracurricular activities, including sports, as long as they enroll part-time.
- California and West Virginia prohibit homeschoolers from playing on public school teams.
- Hawaii, Kansas, Kentucky, New Jersey, Texas, Virginia, and Washington let individual schools decide if homeschoolers can participate in these activities, since they don't have a law granting homeschoolers this privilege.

Check CRHE website for updated requirements.

MUSIC, THEATER, AND ART

Developing the left side of the brain can be accomplished by learning a musical instrument. Learning music can also be socially advantageous to children, especially since there is a relationship between music and language development.

During the 2013 annual neuroscience meeting, Gottfried Schlaug, M.D., Ph.D., a brain plasticity expert from Harvard Medical School, presented research showing that musical training affects the structure and function of different regions of the brain and explains how those regions communicate as music is created. Dr. Schlaug stressed that "intense musical training generates new processes within the brain, at different stages of life, and with a range of impacts on creativity, cognition, and learning. Listening to and making music combines the auditory, multisensory, and motor experience. Making music over a long period of time can change brain function and brain structure."

The least expensive way to expose children to music is to borrow CDs from the library or listen to the radio. Mozart, Beethoven, and Bach were some of our favorite composers. Country, folk, opera, Brazilian, and Spanish music were also explored with discussions of each artist's work and biography.

My children learned how to play guitar at a young age. I remember my younger son not being able to reach the cords, because his hands were too small. However, he enthusiastically sat through his elder brother's guitar lessons eager to play; luckily, the music teacher found ways around the problem. They both were able to play Led Zeppelin, Elton John, and other artists' songs by the time they were 10 years old.

Spend time assisting children develop special talents, including music, drawing, photography, video creation, and programming.

Theater

While a public school's main focus is often on test results, homeschoolers participate in culturally enriching field trips on a regular basis. Field trips enable homeschool students to enhance vocabulary, exposing them to diversity and tolerance to others. Comedy reduces stress and endorses positive behavior. Theatrical plays expose students to situations outside their own lives.

Our homeschool group arranged field trips to plays at local theaters at least once a month. Rates were reasonable, since we went to matinee performances. The impressive New Shanghai Circus should not be missed. Contortionists, tumblers, human pyramids of twisted bodies, and balancing acts on wires were remarkable. Acts such as a woman folding her slim body inside a narrow drum or a tumbling section with men leaping and twisting through hoops were beautifully coordinated, and the precision and physical ability of these performers were incredible.

Historical plays are educational and offer homeschool parents immeasurable opportunities to create lesson plans based on the history of that time period.

Drawing and painting

Since children can't always express themselves with words, drawings and paintings can enhance emotional intellect and creativity; in addition, they improve hand-eye coordination, creating a physical representation of what they are thinking.

Teach children to create perspective (an illusion of three-dimensions) and play with the lighting in drawings. We held our lessons at a local state park and used watercolor paint, pencils, and other art supplies. Drawing books are great assets because they show how to draw people, wild animals, and landscape. The HB pencil creates a rough sketch, the B pencil is used to develop line drawing, and the 3B and 5B pencils produce light-hearted effects.

The book, *Drawing: Landscapes with William Powell*, shows how to create shading techniques, surfaces and textures, landscape composition, perspective, clouds, rocks, trees, structures, mountains, deserts, creeks, and rocks. Learn how to create a sense of depth through perspective by using a range of drawing media.

The animation series by Preston Blair provides step-by-step explanations of how to create animated cartoons and shows how to create facial expressions, movement of bodies, and hand construction. Private art lessons are offered at local art museums or art stores, if children want to improve their skills.

TYPING

Most schools offer typing as an elective in high school. Students, however, should be exposed to this skill much earlier. Touch-typing, contrary to the hunt-and-peck method, enhances speed and accuracy. My sons learned how to type when they were in elementary school, using Mavis Beacon Teaches Typing software. The SpongeBob SquarePants version is optimum for elementary school students. These are interactive and fully customized programs that keep track of a student's progress by measuring accuracy and speed. After tracking errors, it suggests games that focus on specific problem areas. Students can adjust background music, turn off sound, and select what drills or games to play.

Games can be played by clicking on the Game Room that focuses on specific typing skills, such as speed, accuracy, or rhythm. Students can practice typing numbers by using the checkout time game. In the road race game, students must type quickly to stay ahead of other cars. Practice speed with the shark attack game, but make a mistake and bugs will splatter on the windshield. On the penguin afloat game, type the correct words to stay afloat.

By the time they were in middle school, they could easily type reports and emails.

EDUCATIONAL TELEVISION SHOWS

Educational shows expose children to footage that they may not see in real life. They are backed by high-quality developmental principles and expose children to different cultures, thereby stimulating learning.

Movies that are based on novels are great assets for reluctant readers. They give parents the opportunity to have discussions on the differences between the book and movie, which is a great way to build analytical skill. Ensure that these movies or shows are enriching children's education and use these topics to generate valuable discussions.

History Channel, PBS, Discovery Channel, and Science Channel are invaluable resources to enhance your children's education.

- **HowStuffWorks.com** is an infotainment website that shows how the world goes 'round. Videos from Discovery Channel show students can watch how rubber is made and iron is mined, and they can follow the journey of corn and wheat, and water and salt from the ground to the dinner table.
  The show on antibiotics is interesting and informative, and explains how before antibiotics, people had to wait for an infection to improve on its own. Students learn who discovered antibiotics and the difference between bacterial and viral infections.

- **Against the Elements (Science Channel)**
  Explores disasters, both manmade and those found in nature (from hurricanes to floods, mudslides, and fires). Reveals how disasters affect lives and communities around the world.

- **How It's Made (Science Channel)**
  Explores different products that facilitate our everyday life. From hockey pucks and handsaws to drill bits. Have you ever

questioned how aluminum ladders, firefighter helmets, matches, and engine blocks are constructed? The show's host visits assembly lines where raw materials become finished products.

- **How the States Got Their Shape (History Channel)**
  Brian Unger uncovers the history hidden in the contours that created the U.S. map. Contestants compete to win cash and demonstrate their knowledge of U.S. geography as they expose how each state's contour was defined.

These shows are not a replacement for a well-thought-out curriculum; they are meant to enhance your children's education.

CHAPTER FOURTEEN

ELECTIVES LINKED TO CAREER CHOICES

ACCORDING TO THE NATIONAL CENTER of Education Statistics, 80 percent of students change majors at least once. Indecisiveness can lead to additional college debt and longer time to graduate. University admissions committees prefer students who have demonstrated interest in a specific field. Granted, college students do not always have to declare a major in the first two years; however, stress related to this uncertainty causes many students to drop out of college. Candidates have a better chance of getting into Ivy League schools if they have chosen their field of study and demonstrate passion for their subject area when writing their personal statement, with examples of shadowing and volunteering experiences.

Strategies, such as defining students' interests and developing career learning lesson plans, while they are still in middle and high school, helps ensure they get accepted into top universities. Homeschoolers have the freedom to explore subjects that cover different fields of study; however, working with students while they are still in middle and high school is paramount.

MAIN REASONS STUDENTS DROP OUT OF COLLEGE

Students' main reasons for dropping out of college are financial hardship, poor high school preparation, or inability to define a major. Embedding career learning lesson plans into your curriculum and having students shadow professionals help prepare them for a successful college experience.

I have given advice to many college students and parents regarding educational choices and provided assistance with college class selection. None of these students were homeschooled and they all came from different brick-and-mortar schools. Some were indecisive about their major and wanted to take as many classes as they could in the first two years, in hopes of defining their career path. This is simply not a good strategy, because it could add years to college and the cost would be prohibitive. In addition, college students do not have access to higher-level classes that would give them a true measure of what each profession would entail. Classes are similar for every major in the first year since everyone has to take composition, math, and science. In the second year, required classes diverge somewhat depending on student majors. Engineering majors, for example, are required to take Calculus I and II; biology students take Organic Chemistry.

Counselors rigorously work with students to help them define a major. Not all universities offer this service, but some counselors review students' high school transcripts to determine what subjects they excel in and link professions that are in line with their strengths and then suggest courses. This process may take a while and the level of advice students receive varies, depending on the university. So, in reality students only have one year to decide on their major, which can be a stressful ordeal causing many of them to drop out.

In summary, the best solution to avoid this situation is to prepare students in middle and high school and expose them to different professions, shadowing, and volunteering opportunities.

Should counselors or parents discourage students who are not strong in math, but insist on becoming engineers? Students have the opportunity to take remedial math classes in college, so they should take their best shot before giving up on their dream.

CORRELATE HIGH SCHOOL ELECTIVES TO COLLEGE MAJOR

Homeschooling gives students the opportunity to be exposed to many disciplines, allowing them to be prepared to declare a major before entering college. Children's personal interests change over time and being exposed to different activities helps uncover new talents. As early as middle school, parents should listen to their children and find out what intrigues them. Use college catalogs and other resources to research and read about different occupations. Create lesson plans to learn about career choices. Help your children develop their special talents by working on activities that truly inspire them. This exercise will have a significant impact on their development and assist in identifying electives that benefit them. By the end of middle school, parents and students should have narrowed down some of their career choices, which will facilitate choosing electives for high school.

For students who are set on a major early on, electives and lesson plans can be tailored to their career aspirations. In addition, choose supplementary electives that broaden their horizons and introduce them to new professions.

Once students show interest in a specific major, use the following strategies:

- Explore classes related to their field, allowing them to link subjects learned in middle and high school to their major and, as a result, work harder.
- Adapt your teaching methods to incorporate their passion. Through an interactive process, constantly reassess their interest to ensure it is still in line with your curriculum choices and adjust, if necessary.
- Make sure to cater and customize your lessons to each student's interest.
- If children express interest in a profession that you disapprove of, still explore it. They may not be mature enough to define a career, but being exposed to different professions helps narrow down career choices.

Have students volunteer or shadow for different organizations.

SHADOWING AND VOLUNTEERING OPPORTUNITIES

Job shadowing offers hands-on experience to explore different fields. In the first year of high school, students should have been exposed to career choices and have one or several options to explore. Develop a student's career aspirations by searching for volunteering or shadowing opportunities. Shadowing a professional can help students decide if that occupation is a good match for them.

Although student volunteers may not always get to tag along with a professional, it can be a valuable experience that enables them to make better-informed decisions. Volunteering provides networking opportunities, develops new skills, and allows students to meet high school and college requirements. Send out a resume to prospective businesses, along with a letter requesting an opportunity to shadow.

When my older son was in sixth grade, he wanted to be a medical doctor. By seventh grade, he had already volunteered at Holy Cross Hospital and shadowed an orthopedic surgeon. He had also volunteered for many organizations, putting in hundreds of volunteering hours. After his experience in the medical field, his career choice changed. He realized that doctors helped one patient at a time and he felt that neuroscience research would be a better fit for him. He wanted to help discover cures for diseases that affected millions of people. A family member was in the beginning stages of Alzheimer's and maybe that influenced his decision. Since it was impossible to get a research position at that age, he decided to shadow a general pediatrician. The doctor requested that he read a book related to neurological disorders and had discussions with him about the subject. After a few months of shadowing, the doctor asked my son to diagnose a patient. The doctor asked the patient some questions and asked my son if he knew what he had. To the doctor's surprise, my son identified the neurological disorder.

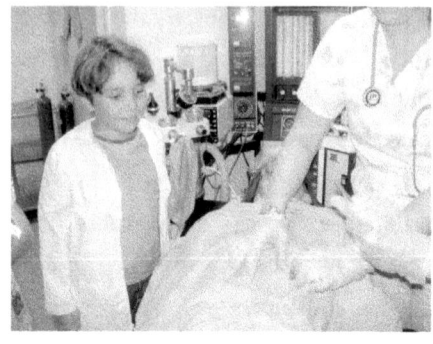

We concentrated his studies in biology and anatomy for middle and high school, since he showed an interest in those topics. He explored the human body using interactive tools from the Internet and played anatomy games. He studied the digestive, respiratory, circulatory, lymphatic, endocrine, urinary, and nervous systems.

He spent hours reading about neuroscience researches done by universities across the country. During his college interview, he was able to explain exactly what area of study he was interested in and what type of research he wanted to do. He was able to cite researches done by university professors and why he found them interesting. His personal statement highlighted his passion and knowledge about the subject. A strong college application shows that a student has a clear interest in a specific area of study. My son's passion for this field never changed, and he has done neuroscience research for Harvard Medical School since he was 19 years old.

How to deal with children with different interests? Electives should be tailored to each individual child. My younger son became interested in engineering when he was in elementary school after visiting Motorola each year during "bring your kid to work day." He was fascinated with the two-way radio and cell phone factory, engineering tools, and cafeteria. Why cafeteria? When anyone asked why he wanted to be an engineer, he would say that it was because he liked the food in the cafeteria at Motorola.

He was exposed to engineering meetings, where he would sit quietly and take notes as the meeting progressed. His electives for middle and high school were science, electronics, physics, and robotics. He designed power supplies, programmed robots, designed websites, RC car alarms, and solar cars. He graduated as an electrical engineer at age 19.

Nurture children's interests by giving them freedom to explore different hobbies as well. Some electives we chose for middle and high school that were outside of their career choice were guitar, career research, economics, civics, Portuguese, Spanish, CPR training, web design, video game development, music production, public speaking, typing, novel writing, and current events.

MIDDLE AND HIGH SCHOOL ELECTIVES

Although every state has its own requirements for high school graduation, core classes are usually pretty similar because universities set these requirements. Standard requirements for most universities are four years of English, two to three years of a foreign language, three years of mathematics, two to three years of science, two to three years of social studies/history, and one year of art. Even though students provide universities with transcripts that include GPA, universities often recalculate students' GPA using core subjects.

Electives should be chosen based on a student's major with a few outside the area of study. Homeschool parents have plenty of opportunities for curriculum customization. While core classes demonstrate a student's academic ability, electives introduce students to topics that may trigger a passion for a future career. Due to the endless array of electives to choose from, some research is needed.

Traditional school students are required to take 8.5 electives and homeschoolers usually follow suit. Each class is worth one credit; however, certain electives are only half a credit. Some of the most popular electives are foreign language, public speaking, personal finance, and computer programming. Personal finance is a high school elective, which we already had covered in middle school. They learned about checking and savings accounts, the importance of saving for retirement (401K and pension), all types of insurance (house, car, medical, and life), credit score, and house and car loans. They applied for their first credit card when they were 15 years old as authorized users on our account. Bank of America, Citi, Wells Fargo, Capital One, and Chase do not have a minimum age requirement. Having a credit card at a young age teaches children responsibility and helps establish credit. Some banks do not report authorized users to the credit bureau, helping credit history.

Homeschoolers can search for electives in the school's course catalog available online. Electives can be taken through virtual or private schools or planned and taught by parents. Students may benefit from taking some of the science electives through an accredited school that offers AP or honors classes to show universities they had a rigorous course load.

Elective options by categories:

- Business: Personal finance, marketing, entrepreneurial skills, accounting, business law and management, and consumer education.

- Physical Education: Pilates, sports, weight training, yoga, health, dance, and aerobics.

- Computer Science: Computer repair, word processing, web design, music production, graphic design, film production, audio production, typing, video game development, animation, app development, and computer programming.

- Foreign Language: Any language.

- Language and Writing: Advanced composition, British literature, humanities, journalism, poetry, public speaking, African literature, and writing.

- Mathematics: Any higher-level math, other than that required for high school.

- Visual Arts: Art history, 3-D art, drawing, film production, painting, jewelry design, sculpture, printmaking, ceramics, digital media, and photography.

- Performing Arts: Dance, guitar, choir, band, drama, music, piano, theater, orchestra, music theory, and jazz band.

- Science: Biotechnology, earth science, environmental science, geology, meteorology, physics, zoology, sound and acoustics, astronomy, marine biology, and agriculture.
- Social Studies: Latin American studies, philosophy, religion, sociology, U.S. government, politics, economics, civics, current events, African, and Asian studies.
- Family and Consumer Science: CPR, early childhood development, chemistry of foods, culinary arts, family studies, fashion, interior design, nutrition, and home economics.
- Vocational Education: Electronics, driver education, criminal justice, auto body repair, building construction, cosmetology, metal working, plumbing, networking, robotics, woodworking, and so many more.

Traditional schools offer only a small portion of these electives; however, homeschoolers will be able to find curriculum for any of the options above.

CHAPTER FIFTEEN

OUTSIDE RESOURCES TO HELP ALLEVIATE STRESS

PARENTS WHO FEEL OVERWHELMED or unqualified to teach specific subject areas can still homeschool and use outside services to alleviate stress. Doubting your ability to teach or second-guessing if homeschooling is the right decision for your child is something that parents experience eventually.

SECOND-GUESSING YOUR ABILITY TO HOMESCHOOL

Homeschool parents tend to second-guess their ability to teach and with so many options available, they often question themselves. Should I use a co-op group? Do universities accept all the classes taught by a parent? Should classes be taken through a private school? What is the benefit of joining an umbrella school? Will my children obtain a high school diploma? Should my children take core subjects through an accredited high school? I answer these questions in the next two chapters.

Questioning yourself makes you reflect on the best options for your family. Just as any homeschool parent, I was not immune to second-guessing myself. Even after I was considered a seasoned homeschool mom, I would still research

Outside Resources to Help Alleviate Stress

the latest curriculums and ways to improve our homeschool experience. The purpose of this book is to present information on each choice, so that homeschool parents can make the right decision for their children.

If your doubt arises due to lack of confidence or time, the options below may help relieve some of the pressure.

My main concern was teaching American History, since I grew up in Brazil and learned mostly Latin American History. Although I took two American History classes at the university, my husband and I decided he should be the one to teach history to our sons.

What kept me up at night?

Anxiety kept me awake many nights. I often wondered if homeschooling was the right decision for our family. Although I was concerned that my sons would not have the same opportunities as other students, my husband had full confidence that we had made the right choice and that I was the most qualified to teach our children.

Knowing that my sons would not have a high school diploma or a transcript with an accredited school seal on it was a concern to me. I belonged to a local homeschool group with thousands of homeschool families, so this was a great platform to begin getting answers. I started my research by asking parents if they knew of any homeschooler who got accepted into an Ivy League university without taking any accredited high school classes. Emails came in from students going to community colleges to those getting accepted into top universities. My conclusion was that most students who got accepted into a decent university had taken dual enrollment classes or high school classes through an accredited high school. My next step was to conduct an investigation to ensure that our academic decisions were in line with local universities' expectations. In addition, if for some reason we had to put our kids back in school, would the high school classes taken through their middle school years be accepted?

I called a few local high schools asking if they accepted homeschoolers. The school counselor at a private catholic school was receptive and emphasized that they loved homeschoolers and that she had homeschooled her own children. "Great, somebody who actually understands the benefits of homeschooling," I thought. I informed her that my son had just finished Algebra I and asked if I would have any problem transferring the credits, since it was a high school class and he was still in sixth grade. The answer was puzzling, "Of course, as long as it was taken through an accredited institution." I thought to myself, "An accredited institution?" So, just in case she did not hear what I had said earlier, I repeated "As I mentioned earlier, my son is homeschooled…" She said that all high school classes would have to be taken through an accredited school or the student would have to take a test for each high school class before being able to transfer the credits. I felt that taking a test four years later would be out of the question. Consequently, we decided to sign our son up with an online school, Seton Home Study School, for Algebra II. This same accredited school allowed us to sign him up for Algebra I as long as he took all 12 tests to be sent and graded by them.

Three universities gave us the same answer. Since my elder son took Algebra I in sixth grade, Algebra II in seventh, and Geometry in eighth, it meant that he would have to take tests on these subjects six years later.

Keep in mind that if a student takes English 101, algebra and geometry classes as a dual enrollment student at a local university while still in high school or acquires an associate degree by the end of 12th grade, getting accepted into a highly selective university will not be an issue. The problem was my son was only 12 years old when I started conducting research, and I did not know if he would be mature enough to take college classes at such a young age.

Homeschooling through high school would be stressful, especially if I wanted to ensure all the classes would be transferable. Of course, if the decision is to homeschool through high school, there are steps that can be taken to ensure your children will have a chance to enter a first-rate university. Contact the universities of your choice and request information on what is required of homeschoolers.

Florida Virtual School (FLVS) and Seton Home Study School are fully accredited and they both offer AP and honors courses for high school students. They also allow middle school students to take higher-level classes. Seton is extremely flexible, compared to FLVS. Tests are sent quarterly and graded by their teachers. The parent can still be the one to teach, but Seton requires the student finish the class in one year.

When should you choose an umbrella school, join a co-op, take an online class, enroll in a private school, or take dual enrollment classes? More information on online classes and required tests is covered in the next chapter.

UMBRELLA SCHOOLS

Although a small number of states require homeschool students to be under an umbrella school or that parents be certified teachers, Florida does not. Parents in the state of Florida can teach their own children and select their own curriculum. Check directly with your state's Department of Education website for additional information on whether parents can choose their own curriculum.

In the beginning of our homeschool journey, we joined an umbrella school. There were some advantages to joining; however, the disadvantages outweighed the benefits. Umbrella schools maintain attendance records, issue report cards, and assist with documentation. Some allow parents to be responsible for the choice of curriculum and for teaching their own children. Umbrella schools may require the child to be registered with the county, offer transcripts, materials, high school diploma, and are accredited.

Why would I not use these schools, since they provide so many benefits?

- Some umbrella schools are considered private schools and students may not be able to participate in extracurricular activities at their local school.

- They may require a health examination and immunization forms, which may be a disadvantage to some parents.

- If the school does not have an articulation agreement with local universities or online schools, students are not allowed to sign up for free classes. An articulation agreement is designed to ensure a seamless transfer between school and university or community college and university.

- The annual standardized test required for homeschoolers by the school board may be waived.

When I called a couple of universities requesting information on dual enrollment, I realized that my sons were not considered homeschoolers and were not allowed to dual enroll and take free college classes. Unfortunately, they were under an umbrella school that did not have an agreement with the local university, which disqualified them for the program. Luckily, we were able to correct the problem by changing their status.

> *Our family had homeschooled in four different states: PA, NV, CA, and FL. My favorite by far was California because they offer homeschool charter options, which is called independent study charters. They pull money from our local public schools and give an educational fund of $1800 per student. We did state testing and checked in once a month with a homeschool friendly evaluator. Every state should offer this option. We had the choice to receive the funds and be evaluated or not be required to be evaluated if we chose not to receive any money.*
>
> *Our least favorite was the state of Pennsylvania because we were forced to jump through hoops to stay legal. This is why we chose to use an umbrella school in Florida.*
>
> **Al. K. (Florida)**

This umbrella school did not require a standardized test; however, we did not perceive that as a benefit. We saw the value of using standardized tests as a diagnostic tool to improve our curriculum. Make sure to ask the right question if you're considering joining an umbrella school.

Finally, if a child is registered with the home education program and wants to sign up with an umbrella school, a notice of termination must be sent to the school board.

Again, this is only true if the umbrella school is considered a private school. A considerably large number of homeschoolers use these services and are happy with their decision. Use caution when choosing the right program for your family. All universities accept homeschoolers and sometimes joining an umbrella school can hurt the student's chance to get into a good university.

CO-OPS

A homeschool co-op is generally where homeschool families get together and each parent teaches a specific subject. Parents may be scientists, teachers, computer programmers, architects, or just a really dedicated, knowledgeable parent who is willing to teach. Co-ops require parents to participate in teaching, become a board member, or organize field trips. They find ways to take advantage of each parent's unique talent to enhance the curriculum. Some co-ops do hire certified teachers to teach their core classes.

Although the structure and rules vary from group to group, organized co-ops do establish guidelines for behavior, set student and parent responsibilities, and establish a dress code. Co-ops can meet a few times a week or every other week. Parents organize field trips once or twice a month.

Although there are benefits in joining a co-op group, there are also drawbacks.

- Choosing the curriculum becomes complicated, since a group of parents from different homeschooling philosophies are involved in the decision making.
- Parents may choose classes that are not your priority, such as acting, drawing, or music.
- If your child is a quick learner, he or she may have to wait for other students to learn the concept. In a way, it defeats the purpose of homeschool.
- The children's ages can be years apart and although that could benefit younger students, older students may become discouraged and bored being in a class with much younger students.
- Time spent commuting to and from the co-op location takes time away from learning or participating in fun activities.

PRIVATE SCHOOLS IN COLLABORATION WITH HOMESCHOOLERS

A Christian school in my area offers classes for homeschoolers twice a week, from kindergarten through eighth grade. The homeschooler can participate in the program by paying a portion of the annual tuition. They teach religion, language arts, mathematics, and history. One of the benefits in joining this program is that students are allowed to participate in sports and band with full-time students. The curriculum is pretty set; however, a placement test determines the student's math level. The problem was that the highest class they offered was Algebra I; as a result, a more advanced student would not benefit from this program.

ENRICHMENT HOMESCHOOL CLASSES

These are schools created by homeschool parents. Although classes are occasionally taught by teachers, the schools are not accredited and do not offer a high school diploma. They offer math, science, English, Spanish, and social studies. They encourage dual enrollment and advice on college enrollment and scholarships. Private tutoring, guidance counselor, transcript preparation, SAT and PSAT prep classes may also be offered by these schools.

Should you hire an instructor? For parents who feel unqualified to tutor a specific subject, hiring an instructor is an option to fill the gap and speed up the learning process. Students can also join a co-op group or sign up with a private school that offers part-time teaching instructions for homeschoolers.

SUPPORT GROUPS

A support group is usually composed of volunteer homeschool parents who dedicate their time to provide information to other homeschoolers. They organize field trips and social enrichment programs throughout the year. Groups can be Christian-based or all-inclusive and offer activities that cater to teenagers only.

Homeschool families have the choice of being a member of one or more support groups. These groups bring guest speakers to their monthly meetings, generate student ID, organize dance nights, publish yearbooks, plan park days, offer educational co-ops, plan high school proms, organize spelling and geography bees, participate in science fairs, offer standardized testing, have used curriculum/book sales, and plan yearly graduation ceremonies. Parents can also obtain a teacher's ID, which is useful for discounts on books and other merchandise. For example, Barnes & Noble offers homeschool parents a 20 percent discount card; however, the card needs to be renewed once a year.

CHAPTER SIXTEEN

PREPARING FOR COLLEGE

COLLEGE PREPARATION SHOULD START in middle school. Chapter eight covered detailed information on how to choose the right curriculum, taking into account each state's requirements. Add career exploration lesson plans in middle school. The best chance for students to be successful in college is to develop a plan that works backwards from their career goal. It is never too early to contact universities and ask questions.

Some parents believe that if universities are not homeschool friendly, they just have to explain the legality of their choice, and as long as they provide homeschool law articles, the university will not ask questions. Applying for college by claiming your rights is hardly a good start, and it does not guarantee good results. If your children are academically prepared, there should be no reason for stress.

Classes chosen for middle school may not seem important because universities do not look at middle school transcripts; however, many decisions should be made during the middle school years. Students can start thinking of a career choice by eighth grade.

CAREER GOAL

Traditional versus accredited homeschooler

Homeschooled students generally fall into two categories: traditional or accredited.

- Traditional homeschoolers: Students who have not taken high school classes through accredited institutions and will not have an official transcript when applying for college.
  In this case, universities will put more emphasis on SAT or ACT scores during the admission process.
- Accredited homeschoolers: Students who have taken high school classes through accredited institutions or dual enrollment classes at a local college or university.

Although every university has different rules, most consider students who have taken a minimum of 15 credits through an accredited school to be assessed the same as incoming freshmen from traditional schools.

Try to avoid extra challenges when applying to college by considering an "accredited" homeschool option or search for colleges that are considered "home-school friendly." Research university requirements and plan ahead. As early as middle school, I contacted admission offices at two universities to ensure that we were making the correct curriculum choices. Unfortunately, my research showed that universities were not as receptive in accepting "traditional" homeschoolers as I was led to believe (Chapter 15). University of Florida and Florida Atlantic University stressed that they would not accept high school classes that were not taken through accredited schools and, in addition, SAT subject tests would be required for core classes. Due to rigorous admissions requirements, I needed to change my plan. To avoid taking a test six years after the fact, high school classes had to be retaken through accredited schools. There are many options available; however, we chose Seton Home Study School, a catholic high school, which is SACs accredited. Southern Association of Colleges and Schools (SACs) is one of the six regional accreditations that monitors and evaluates educational institutions.

Algebra I was taken in sixth grade, Algebra II in seventh, and Geometry in eighth. Although parents still teach each class, the school assigns a certified teacher to each student. The teacher administers and grades all tests and is available if students have any questions, although my sons never used their service.

Solutions to ensure a successful transition

As mentioned earlier, universities treat students who take 15 or more hours of dual enrollment classes the same as if they were traditional school students. If that is not an option, private schools and public schools offer classes to homeschoolers. Some universities required SAT subject tests from all incoming freshmen. For example, USC required homeschoolers to take the SAT subject exam for math, in addition to SAT or ACT tests. Subject Tests helped admissions officers compare students and helped homeschoolers demonstrate their abilities in a specific field of study. Universities will be adjusting their policies this year, but homeschoolers should consider AP (or IB) exams in lieu of Subject Tests to give them a competitive advantage. Before deciding which classes to take through an accredited institution, check what universities require.

Dual enrollment at a local community college or university: Once a letter of intent to homeschool is sent to the superintendent's office, the student is considered a homeschooler and can sign up for college classes. If your child is registered with an umbrella school that has an articulation agreement with local universities, dual enrollment is free in Florida, and students only have to purchase textbooks. For more information on which states offer "FREE" dual enrollment classes, go to FromHomeschoolToHarvard.com.

Sign up for online high school classes: There are many options for online public and private schools; however, make sure you choose one that allows some flexibility.

Some states require an end of course (EOC) assessment test for core classes, and a minimum grade is required to pass. In Florida, it is a requirement to take the EOC for Algebra I, Biology, and American History (chapter five). Tests are added to the list every year, so check with the school board to find out which tests are required. These three-hour-long multiple-choice tests are only required if students take high school classes through online public schools. These schools also offer advanced placement (AP) and honors courses. Another benefit of taking classes outside the home is that online teachers will be able to provide recommendation letters, which are required by universities.

Universities prefer students who have challenged themselves with rigorous study in a range of academic areas during their high school years.

High school diploma or GED

The majority of universities throughout the country require a high school diploma, although some may forego this requirement. Traditional homeschoolers do not earn a high school diploma; however, they can generate their own diploma and transcript. Universities accept parent-issued diplomas; however, some may also request subject SAT tests. Some states, such as New York, have state laws claiming that only public and private schools are allowed to award diplomas. In addition, to be eligible for state financial aid, students have to earn a GED, obtain a letter from the school district demonstrating that their education was similar to public school education, or take an ability-to-benefit test (Pearson, ACT, SLET, The College Board, or WBST).

Disadvantages of getting a General Educational Development diploma (GED):

- State scholarships do not treat students with a GED diploma the same as homeschoolers or students who graduated from public or private schools. A GED recipient may be eligible to receive a smaller scholarship amount, compared to a homeschooler with a parent-issued diploma. Homeschoolers qualify for need-basis scholarships and federal financial aid (FAFSA).
- A GED may not be the best option for college-bound students; however, it may be the only option for employment. An employer pays GED recipients less.
- Does the military require a diploma? There are three tiers of enlistment and GED recipients fall into the second tier, while a homeschooler falls into tier one at a higher salary. A homemade diploma and a transcript are needed for homeschoolers to enlist as tier one, as long as the student's parents provided the education.
- University admission offices do not regard a GED diploma equivalent to a regular high school diploma and may even consider it inferior; however, students are eligible for financial aid. If a GED is required for admission, find a different option because it may hurt your child's possibilities of applying to different universities. Every college has different policies and some are more homeschool friendly than others.

Many private schools offer nationally accredited programs where students can earn a high school diploma; however, they may have to take full-time classes with them and the curriculum will not cater to your child's individual needs. Depending on the school, the student may no longer be considered homeschooled.

Some states, such as North Dakota, allow homeschool students to earn a diploma from their local public school. However, the school board determines subjects required and number of hours parents should teach. Students also have to take all additional tests required for public school students.

Pennsylvania homeschoolers' diplomas are provided by Pennsylvania's Department of Education. The program specifies how many hours and what to teach. It is wise to research if your state has similar opportunities.

Be aware of schools, private or umbrella, that claim to offer a high school diploma. Most umbrella schools are not accredited and having a diploma from those schools may hurt students' chances of getting into top universities. On the other hand, private schools that are accredited will more likely provide the curriculum and require most classes be taken through them. That will add to cost and students will no longer be considered homeschoolers.

Do all universities require an accredited high school diploma?

Accredited schools meet "standards of qualification" set by an accrediting agency and guarantee continuous improvement. They provide safe environments, qualified teachers, rigorous curriculum, student activities, and credits can be transferred from school to school. Diplomas are accepted by universities, employers, and military.

Even though we were homeschooling our children, we were not sure if our sons would attend a brick-and-mortar high school in the future, so we wanted to leave our options open. The safest path when planning high school classes is to ensure that core classes (English, science, and math) are taken through an accredited school. All universities in the United States accept accreditations from the Regional Accreditation agencies listed below. There are other accreditations, but most universities only accept these.

Regional Accreditation Agencies

- Middle States Commission on Higher Education (MSCHE)
- New England Association of Schools and Colleges (NECHE)
- New England Association of Schools and Colleges (NEASC CTCI)
- North Central Association Commission on Accreditation and School Improvement (NCA CASI)
- North Central Association of Colleges and Schools Higher Learning Commission (NCACS HLC)
- Northwest Commission on Collleges and Universities (NWCCU)

- Southern Association of Colleges and Schools Commission on Colleges (SACS COC)
- Western Association of Schools and Colleges Accrediting Commission for Community and Junior Colleges (WASC ACCJC)
- Western Association of Schools and Colleges Accrediting Commission for Schools (WASC ACS)
- Western Association of Schools and Colleges Accrediting Commission for Senior Colleges and Universities (WASC ACSCU)

Requirements may vary across the country:

- University of Denver accepts the accreditations above, plus the National Council for Private School Accreditation (NCPSA).
- MIT does not require a high school diploma. They require the SAT or ACT test and students no longer have to take SAT subject tests for math and science.
- Perdue University claims they accept all schools, no matter what accreditation.

As demonstrated above, requirements for each university vary greatly.

Preparing a homeschool transcript

A transcript is an inventory of a student's course work. Homeschool parents can prepare their own middle and high school transcripts, which should include student's personal information, academic history, attendance records, final grades for each subject, cumulative GPA, and extracurricular activities. Keeping a transcript is essential for college-bound students.

I have included a blank transcript template, with detailed information, on my website FromHomeschoolToHarvard.com. Follow the template to create a transcript for your children. I also added information on how to calculate a student's weighted and unweighted GPA.

1. I wrote "Official School Record" on the top left corner of the header of the transcript. Why? Most universities require an official transcript; therefore, I decided to make it official just by adding this disclaimer. To clarify, the meaning of an official

transcript is that it is provided by an accredited institution. Since my sons took all high school classes through schools that were SACs accredited, while they were in middle school, and each school transcript was attached to my "homemade" transcript, it was appropriate. Although I did not choose this option, some homeschool transcripts may cite student's state homeschool law on it (Education completed in accordance with Florida Department of Education law and law number). Another option is to have a copy of your state's homeschooling law ready to show the admission's office, if necessary. The superintendent's office, in some states, will provide a letter stating that the student's education was compliant with the law.

2. My husband and I signed the transcript and had it notarized.
3. Cumulative GPA, which is an average from ninth to 12th grade, should also be included.

Most umbrella schools or correspondence schools provide students with a transcript. Unless the school is accredited by a regional accreditation agency, accepted by universities throughout the country, the transcript is as good as a parent-prepared curriculum. Students would be better off making their own transcript, rather than providing universities with a transcript from a non-accredited institution. Students who take classes through online or accredited school should request a copy of the transcript from those institutions and attach it to their homemade transcript.

What is unweighted and weighted GPA? Grade point average is the average of all a student's grades for high school classes.

- **Unweighted GPA**: Means that all classes get the same weight, even if the student takes honors, advanced placement (AP), or dual enrollment classes. The scale goes from zero (F) to four (A).
- **Weighted GPA**: Classes do not get the same numerical value. AP, honors, and dual enrollment classes weigh more heavily (regular class range from zero to four, honors classes from zero to four and a half, AP classes from zero to five, and dual enrollment from zero to six.)

Since not all schools offer AP or honors classes, *unweighted GPA* is the only way for colleges to compare students throughout the United States. Universities often suggest that students select rigorous classes, but do not penalize students who attend schools that do not offer those options.

Here is a simple example for calculating GPA for four classes. (More detailed information is on my website.)

- School A (offers higher-level classes): A student takes English AP class (worth 0 to 5.0), an honor American History class (worth 0 to 4.5), a dual enrollment class for Art Appreciation (worth 0 to 6.0), and finally a regular Geometry class (worth 0 to 4.0). The student earned an A in all four classes. To calculate the average, we need to translate each grade to a numerical value and then take the average.
  Weighted GPA: 4.87/*Unweighted GPA*: 4.0
- School B (does not offer higher-level classes): A student takes English (worth 0 to 4.0), American History (worth 0 to 4.0), Art Appreciation (worth 0 to 4.0), and finally Geometry (worth 0 to 4.0). The student earned an A in all four classes, as well.
  Weighted GPA: 4.0/*Unweighted GPA*: 4.0

Conclusion: Student from school A has higher *weighted GPA* than the student from school B, even though they both earned an A in all four classes.

You may be wondering why students would take higher-level classes, which are significantly more difficult, if universities compare students using *unweighted GPA*.

- Universities look at the rigor of the courses taken by the student. Honors, AP, and dual enrollment classes signal strong academic skill.
- High scores on AP exams allow students to earn college credits.
- Universities have information on which schools offer rigorous classes; therefore, universities question students' decisions if they chose not to take AP or honors classes.

Earning college credits while in high school

High school students, who are high achievers, have the option of taking advance placement classes. AP is a program created by the College Board, which offers college-level classes to high school students.

College Board, an organization that helps students prepare for college, requires all AP classes to be administered by an accredited school and courses be approved and audited by them. Schools need to be registered with College Board in order to administer exams.

Homeschool educators can request approval for their AP classes by creating an account with College Board and submitting course material along with a course syllabus. After evaluating all documents, the organization will decide if classes meet their requirements. Advanced placement is graded on a simple five-point scale. Each university has their own guideline of which AP classes will be accepted and what grade level is required to earn university credits. Before taking an AP course, check each university's rules. The point-scale for AP exams ranges from one to five, where a "five" means exceptionally qualified and a "one" is not recommended to receive college credits.

With a total of 37 AP courses offered each May around the country, students have a chance to eliminate college classes required for their majors. Remember that homeschoolers can only label courses as "advanced placement" on their high school transcripts if College Board AP Central pre-approves the syllabus. Otherwise, it is illegal to use the AP trademark on the transcript. Attach pre-approved letters for each AP test to the transcript before sending to colleges. Normally, universities will have a list of approved schools; however, College Board chooses not to list approved homeschoolers curriculum, and universities are unable to check if classes are valid. Parents have to contact individual universities and provide them with the College Board approval letter.

Most public and private schools are accommodating and permit homeschooled students to take AP tests in their schools. Our local public school allowed my sons to take the EOC and SAT tests during school hours. Test preparation materials are available online for all AP tests.

CLEP exam

The College-Level Examination Program® (CLEP) allows students to receive three to 12 college credits for subjects already mastered. The cost for each exam is $80, which is a fraction of a college class. Each university has its own rules on accepting CLEP exams results. If a student fails the test, it can be retaken six months later.

Dual enrollment and university requirements

High school students can be enrolled in high school and college concurrently. Dual enrollment classes are offered free of charge to homeschoolers (Florida and

14 other states). This is a great opportunity to earn high school and college credits simultaneously. If the parents' strategy is to homeschool through high school, they should dual enroll at a local university and sign up with an accredited online school for core classes. My younger son took seven high school classes while he was in middle school, all through accredited institutions, and those credits were accepted by Florida Atlantic University.

- Dual enrollment introduces students to the rigors of college coursework; consequently, it is crucial to ensure they are academically prepared and mature enough to handle high-level classes.
- Taking higher-level classes at such a young age enables students to probe their area of academic interest.
- Students may change majors at least once, so the opportunity of taking college classes, while in high school, helps them determine their interests long before they declare a major.
- College admission offices prefer that students take rigorous classes. Dual enrollment classes demonstrate that students can handle difficult coursework.
- College courses augment a student's resume.

Some universities are more selective than others. Due to the growing population, competition has increased for all public and private universities. Although a 4.0 *unweighted GPA* is no longer the only requirement for acceptance into a highly selective university, it is still essential. High SAT or ACT scores, extracurricular activities, leadership skills, class ranking, and volunteer activities also influence college admission.

- **Accelerated classes:** Universities prefer that students sign up for challenging classes such as AP, honors, or dual enrollment.
- **GPA:** Universities seek consistency by ensuring that student's grades were high from the ninth to the 12th grade. Low grades in the first year of high school may also affect chances of admission into college. Illness or other extenuating circumstances that affected student's grades require an explanation. Universities love to see students succeed despite issues.
- **Class ranking:** Since homeschoolers cannot have valedictorian status, they should compensate by participating in activities

that allow them to shine. Joining a debate team, planning and executing a project to help the community are some examples of activities that help homeschoolers stand out.

- **Extracurricular activities:** Universities look for a well-rounded applicant who is involved with nonprofit organizations. They prefer students who participate in clubs or organizations that make an impact, rather than joining numerous organizations with less involvement.

- **Volunteering:** There are innumerable opportunities for volunteering in the community, out of state, or out of the country that can teach children the value of helping less fortunate people and build a sense of responsibility. Schools across the country have instituted community service requirements for middle and high school students. There is a 100-hour community service requirement to graduate high school; nevertheless, homeschoolers exceed those hours since they tend to be more involved in the community. This requirement is necessary if students intend to apply for a Bright Future Scholarship in Florida. Since requirements for scholarships vary from state to state, it is vital to check the rules for your state.
Although most people believe that volunteering plays a big role in college admission, not all colleges consider this as important as other requirements. Princeton University rates volunteering and extracurricular activities a two out of four. Meanwhile, students' GPA and SAT scores are more important. On the other hand, University of Florida rates volunteering four out of four. However, since students do not choose a university until their senior year, it is necessary to meet those requirements in case their university of interest ranks those activities high.

- **Leadership skills:** This was a simple requirement for my sons, since they were Boys Scouts and needed leadership positions in the troop to be promoted to each rank.

- **Letter of reference:** All college applicants are required to submit between two to four letters of reference, depending on the university. Although requirements vary, parents or family members should not submit reference letters. Students who take online classes could request letters from teachers or guidance counselors. Letters from scout leaders or employers are usually accepted, but academic references are mandatory. Letters should contain student's name, how the referrer knows the applicant, student's academic ability, student's greatest strength and weakness, and how the student compares to the rest of the class.

SAT Adversity Score

In Fall 2019, College Board added an adversity score to the SAT test. The number indicates a student's social-economic background, using 15 factors in three categories:

- Neighborhood environment: Includes crime rate, housing values, and poverty rate.
- Family environment: Median income, single-parent household, education level, and ESL.
- High school environment: Curriculum rigor, free lunch rate, and AP opportunity.

College Board's CEO gave various TV interviews about this controversial topic explaining, "There are a number of amazing students who may have scored less on the SAT, but have accomplished more. We can't sit on our hands and ignore the disparities of wealth reflected on the SAT."

Students do not know what score they are given and are assigned an arbitrary number. Fifty universities used this score system in 2018 as a beta test. The SAT is supposed to be an objective measure of students' achievements and a predictor of their ability to succeed in college. Although universities claim that this score provides a more accurate reflection of diversity, life does not give us an adversity score.

Perhaps we could level the playing field for all students and get rid of assignments to the public school by ZIP code, allowing middle and high school students to select the best school available to them. Assigning a number to a student, based on socio-economic background is another way to control a student's fate based on his or her ZIP code.

In August 2019, College Board modified the SAT adversity score rules after listening to their critics, who claim the rules have to be consistent, no matter where students live or what school they attend. Another explanation is that the score may hurt students, from high-crime neighborhoods, who earned scholarships to attend better high schools.

Although the data is still available to university admission offices, adversity information is no longer combined into one score.

Accuplacer, PERT, or Compass tests

In order to dual enroll at a university or community college, students must meet the minimum score required on a placement test prior to admission. Accuplacer, PERT, and Compass Test are some of the options.

The Accuplacer test includes sentence skills, reading comprehension, and math. The math test covers arithmetic, elementary algebra, and college-level math. A sample test is available online. Universities in Florida require students to sign up for the Postsecondary Education Readiness Test (PERT) in order to accurately place them in the right math-level class, according to their abilities.

SAT SUBJECT TESTS

SAT Subject Tests have been discontinued in the United States, but still in effect internationally until June 2021. These tests were required by universities to guarantee that students were ready for college-level courses in specific subject areas. Universities may ask for AP scores in lieu of Subject Tests. AP exams assess a student's college-level knowledge and cover advanced topics in more depth. This policy change could affect applicants who were counting on high SAT test scores to gain competitive advantage, however the AP tests can be a good substitute. Stay informed of future changes to college admissions because these policy changes are possibly the first of many to come.

STANDARDIZED TESTS FOR GRADUATE STUDENTS

Universities in the United States rely on specific standardized tests for higher-level education admission as a tool to objectively compare candidates. The main tests are: TOEFL exam for foreigners; GMAT exam for business school candidates; LSAT exam for law school students; GRE for technical degrees; and MCAT for medical school candidates.

Graduate Record Examination (GRE)

The GRE is used for admissions to all types of master and doctoral programs.

It measures quantitative reasoning, critical thinking, analytical skill, and verbal reasoning. This almost four-hour computerized assessment can be taken worldwide and is valid for five years.

Medical College Admissions Test (MCAT)

This computerized five-and-a-half-hour exam is used for medical school admission. It is designed to test problem-solving skills, science concepts, and writing skills. It is a difficult test that requires substantial preparation.

CHAPTER SEVENTEEN

SOCIAL BEHAVIOR

THERE ARE MANY TECHNIQUES that can be implemented to help modify children's behavior.

Having the will power to modify behavior

A shy person is someone who is uncomfortable with other people and feels anxiety when in proximity with others. Although shyness occurs primarily in unfamiliar surroundings, it can also be triggered by familiar places, such as school. People may form a poor impression of you, since shy people distance themselves from other people.

I always told my children that there is a fine line between shyness, being a snob, or being plain dull. Shy people, or introverts, may not feel comfortable interacting with others; yet it can appear as if they have no desire to interact with others. They are quiet and have a difficult time coming up with topics to talk about; as a result, conversations die quickly. They also may have low self-esteem, making it difficult to succeed. Although changing a person's personality is not an effortless undertaking, it can be accomplished.

There are various characteristics that describe introverts. They may be inhibited, soft spoken, have trouble with self-assertion, exhibit anxiety, or feel mortified when people notice their presence. I was one of those shy people who eagerly desired to adjust my behavior and be more outgoing.

I felt that shyness would limit my career choices and having self-doubt would impact on how well I would perform during a college or job interview. Note, however, that changing your personality requires perseverance.

When I was a teenager, I did not feel comfortable interacting with people. Although I tried not to show it, my exterior mannerisms did not hide my inner turmoil. It appeared that people persistently stared as I attempted to connect with others. Since I did not exhibit traits of an exceedingly shy person, they doubtless believed that I was a snob. Although I had the ability to change my personality, it was not a stress-free task.

When my niece was in elementary school, she showed the same traits I had as a teenager. She was shy and did not have many friends. It is acceptable for people to be shy, as long as they are content with themselves. I noticed, however, that she was not comfortable being that way, and came across as rude when children tried to interact with her. I asked her why she was not playing with other children and she did not have an answer.

Since my sister did not want those traits to follow her daughter into adulthood, she and I had a conversation with her. We discussed that she could be friendly with children at school and that it did not suggest they would be best friends or show up at her house uninvited. However, in order to meet new people, she had to interact with them. Social interaction is a wonderful way to learn about other children and improve social skills.

We stressed that class participation would be part of her grades and her shyness could prevent teachers from getting to know her. As a result, it would be difficult for teachers to write a good recommendation letter, which would be required for high school or college. Shyness can affect a person's career choice and limit promotions for leadership positions. Ordinarily a job promotion results in having extra responsibility, a need to interact with others, and the ability to manage conflicts. It requires extensive effort and it is a considerably more difficult endeavor than just being a single contributor.

We all have the capability to modify our behavior. I did not realize how significant this problem was until a teacher asked my niece to participate in a school event. Her school was celebrating its 50th anniversary and every student had to participate. Students were supposed to move their arms sideways as the music played.

My sister did not speak English well enough to talk with the teacher, so she contacted me, explained that my niece refused to participate, and asked if she should force her to practice the dance. I told her, "absolutely not" and found out later she was uncomfortable making silly gestures. This issue prompted a series of conversations. In the real world, we have to follow directions, and at a job even if we feel deadlines are unreasonable, we do not have a say.

After this incident, my niece decided she needed to change. The first breakthrough came only a few months later when she resolved to play a guitar solo in her school's talent show. When she showed interest in participating, I realized how much this behavior had been bothering her and how much she wanted to change. This shows that perseverance and desire can mold and change someone's behavior.

Dealing with bad behavior

Children act out for attention; therefore, it is imperative to put more emphasis on good behavior and not so much on bad behavior, because, oftentimes, good behavior goes unnoticed. Bad behavior should not be accepted. Parents can change their children's behavior by enticing them to follow rules using strategies personalized for each child. Children can learn to have self-control and not overreact when they don't get their way. Behavior modification, altering one's conduct regardless of the cause, is an excellent method to elicit good behavior. One impactful way to correct bad behavior is to ignore children who are misbehaving and praise children who are not acting out. Whether parents use positive or negative reinforcement to address behavior issues, consistency is vital.

Young children's negative behavior

Set rules for negative behavior, and be flexible enough to modify rules that are not effective. For example, my younger son's worse nightmare was losing video game time as a punishment for bad behavior. My elder son, however, could care less about video games, so I took away his cell phone instead. Children need to understand ahead of time what the consequence of bad behavior will be and how long it will last. Long-term punishment is ineffective, so not having a timeframe for when items will be returned only discourages kids from correcting their behavior. Return objects once behavior is corrected, because removing additional privileges is an ineffective exercise since eventually nothing is left to take away. Positive reinforcement and praise is an effective technique in any household and encourages recurring positive behavior.

Teenage years "The rebellion phase"

Teenage years can be challenging, since this is the time when youths crave independence. Parents frequently wonder how to handle this challenging phase. My dad passed away when I was 3 years old and my loving and caring mom raised my sisters and me. She taught us to be independent and believed that children needed to develop good judgment and learn from mistakes.

She always warned us of consequences if we made the wrong choices. Teaching children core values empowers them to make the right choices. My mom's advice had a profound impact on my life, so when my children were teenagers, I decided to follow her lead.

From the fourth grade on, my children were responsible for their assignments, making new friends, and choosing which activities to participate in. As children mature, allow them to make their own decisions.

Children who are in the third grade or below may not understand that a negative or positive consequence is an outcome of their behavior, so they may still need their parents' assistance in making the right choices. If one of my sons decided to have friends over, instead of working on a project for school, and this choice resulted in a poor grade, he would have to live with the consequences. It is tempting to be a "helicopter" parent and make all your teens' decisions for them; however, this approach only slows down or prevents them from maturing and making better choices. Of course, everything has to be in moderation. When parents feel their child lacks the ability and maturity, they can start the process with something that does not have a significant consequence. For example, tell them they need to be in bed at a certain time and allow them to decide when they need to start getting ready for bed without constantly reminding them.

During their college years, they will not have mom and dad around to help; for that reason, build up this skill early in life. Obviously, the purpose of natural consequence is not to allow children to do something harmful, but parents should avoid hovering. For example, if siblings are playing a game and one of them cheats, as a natural consequence the second player would stop playing and the child who cheated will make the connection between his or her behavior and the consequences.

I hoped our family would be immune to the teenager years, but no. Our sons tried to talk back, tried to discount what we said, and often rolled their eyes. The best, most efficient way to handle bad behavior is to have both parents agree on what is acceptable comportment and discipline accordingly. Teenagers should not be allowed to dismiss what one parent says and reply, "I will ask dad when he returns from work." This only happened a few times in our household, until they figured out that dad would not contradict what I said.

"Teenagers are basically hard-wired to butt heads with their parents," says Stuart Goldman, M.D., director of psychiatric education at Children's Hospital in Boston. Teenagers should never be allowed to talk back and disrespect their parents or cross set boundaries.

Try not to trivialize concerns that teens have. Instead, put everything into perspective and allow them to make their own choices, even if they differ from yours. Some parents do not disapprove of bad behavior, claiming that teens need to express themselves. On the contrary, children need to learn to treat people with respect. When I tell parents that my children were not allowed to play video games during the week, they questioned, "How do you enforce that? I have the same rules and my son refuses to listen." This is puzzling and disturbing.

Children need to follow rules early on and have consequences for not complying. They will not miss playing games or watching TV if they are provided with more interesting activities. They can create their own video games, spend time outdoors, play sports, or learn how to play an instrument. My sons were allowed to watch TV if the shows were in Portuguese, since they were learning the language. Will talk about this topic in more detail in the next chapter and explain how to enforce your rules.

It is important for teens to learn this skill early on because when they become adults, they will have to follow instructions from their employers. Teenage years could be the last few years that your children are under your control, because eventually they will apply to college and get a job. How sad if the last few years with your teenagers turned out to be a nightmare. It is possible to modify their behavior and have a treasured relationship. Conflicts happen when parents fight to suppress children's independence.

Some educators and parents believe that the prefrontal cortex of a teenager is immature and not fully developed until the mid-20s and use this excuse for unacceptable behavior; however, some scientists do not agree that teenagers' brains are different. One psychologist claims that this argument is extremely American-focused, and other cultures don't associate adolescence with a period of extreme angst [Sabbagh 2006]. He suggests that teenage torment is a social influence. In other cultures, teenagers spend plenty of time with adults; consequently, they have more opportunities to learn how to make thoughtful decisions. Teens who are close to their family are more attentive. We had family time at our cabin in the mountains and travelled often.

Teenagers have the desire to show parents they are independent and can think for themselves. They may roll their eyes or give you the "whatever" attitude; but although it is essential for teens to stand up for what they believe in, adults need to set firm boundaries. Not everything needs to turn into an argument.

Identify target behaviors and set goals. Expectations should be clear and rules individualized. Once clear boundaries are set, allow children to present their position regarding the rules. Take their opinion into consideration, before finalizing a "non-acceptable behavior list" and possible repercussions for not following instructions. Be consistent and follow up with the consequences agreed upon. My younger son always tried to negotiate and change our rules because he did not like the consequences. Make it clear that repercussions are final and they can't argue their way out of them. In our house, if they whined, they received a second consequence.

Teenagers are likely to have emotional outbursts due to hormone changes. If they are disrespectful, ask them to rephrase what was said. This is a useful tool to teach how to communicate efficiently. Bad habits that are corrected at a young age help children evolve into productive adults. Having my teens at home during the "attitude phase" was beneficial, since I was able to correct their bad attitude as it occurred.

Homeschool parents become their children's confidant in a time when the norm would be for them to pull away. They share their fears, concerns, and dreams. The pressure of dating can be delayed a few years; after all, there is no peer pressure. Homeschool allows children to develop at their own speed, in their own way and to fulfill their unique potential, away from peers, and to grow into who they are and not what society expects them to be.

Good behavior often goes unnoticed

Children often misbehave in an attempt to gain attention. I always tried to pay special attention to my children when they were following instructions. I praised them often, giving them the incentive to behave the "right way" every time. Children crave attention; consequently, if they are praised for good behavior they receive the attention they are seeking. Instead of giving misbehaved children the attention they seek, praise the children who are behaving appropriately.

When my younger child was misbehaving and acting out, I would compliment my quiet son, reinforcing his positive behavior. Children should know why they are being praised. At school, teachers tend to pay attention to misbehaving children and ignore the ones who are following the rules.

Should we punish all our children if one of them misbehaves?

Punishing the entire classroom for the misdeed of one student is common practice in the school system. Although negative consequences discourage negative behaviors, misbehaving children should not become the focus of attention all the time. Too much attention to negative behavior would inadvertently encourage unacceptable comportment. Ignoring a child with mild misbehavior or not allowing that child to take recess can be considered a negative consequence; however, punishing the entire class is unacceptable.

I have witnessed countless times a teacher humiliating a child for misbehaving. If she'd simply praise the ones who were following the rules, the misbehaving child would imitate the behavior and fight for the same attention.

You may say, "Teachers reinforce positive behavior by giving candy to students who listen to them…" That is true and my son's teacher did exactly that. She tried to reinforce positive behavior with occasional awards or treats. It didn't always work, because some children didn't like the candy she offered, treats were not enticing enough, or they just got accustomed to these treats and didn't appreciate them.

Unfortunately, it is impossible to cater to each student when you have a classroom of 20-plus students. However, homeschool parents can create a system that works for each child. Although the star system (chapter two) does not provide immediate reward, it becomes a competition to compare who earned the most stars. The star system allowed me to create a positive school setting and improve the overall climate of the learning environment, where my children could learn and thrive.

I don't believe in rewarding students with candy for good behavior, due to today's obesity problem.

SOCIAL SKILLS

Watch children as they interact with peers and family members. Good social skills are essential for academic success. Parent-teacher conferences enable parents to find out how their children behave at school, since they may act in a different way when interacting with peers. If they are homeschooled and attend classes outside of the home, ask teachers how your child interacts with other students or if there is a behavior issue. If their comments are too vague, ask for examples to assist you in helping your child at home. Although a teacher's teaching style may be affecting your child's behavior, refrain from blaming him or her. Children have the tendency to justify their behavior by blaming others, but they need to take responsibility for their own decisions and never blame anyone else for their actions.

Allowing them to rationalize their bad actions denies them the opportunity to make the necessary corrections.

Parents can teach children how to behave socially. To ensure that children maintain good relationship with their friends, their character traits need to be polished. For example, play board games with your children and teach them how to be a good sport. My husband taught my children how to play chess when they were 6 years old. He plays fair and never makes it easy for them to win, even if losing upsets them. At first, I felt that he was cruel and even asked him to let them win. He claimed that they had to learn about good sportsmanship, and that they wouldn't win all the time in life either.

Bullying: A student at the elementary school I worked at was diagnosed with pes planus, also known as flat feet, where the arches of the feet collapse. This problem made it difficult, if not impossible, for her to run fast, so her peers bullied her. Children often bully other children in a covert way — below an adult's radar. They made fun of her, and the teachers didn't even notice. After sharing her frustration with me, I immediately spoke to the teacher, and she took care of it. According to the doctor, no treatment was available and only time would change the curvature of her feet. With time, she gained speed and her feet improved and she was able to play sports.

Peer pressure: Although fitting in during adolescence is vital, teenagers need to learn that peer pressure can be indirect, and they don't have to follow the crowd. They can make their own decisions and ensure that they do not contradict their personal standard of conduct.

Role playing: Introduce children to situations they may encounter outside of the home and set the tone for peer interaction. I explained to my children that if a friend tries to persuade them to try drugs or alcohol, they can say NO. Perhaps that friend will ostracize them for not following the crowd; however, their opinion should not matter. True friends will value their opinion and think highly of them for speaking up. If children have a solid foundation at home, they will confidently say no to dangerous situations.

How to never hear "I'm bored" from your children again

Giving children only structured activities denies them the opportunity to explore and be creative. Unstructured activities enable children to explore the world and find out what they have an interest in. My children, not being allowed TV or video gaming during the week, had plenty of time to explore. Try to wean children from TV by reducing screen time and sending them outdoors.

Provide children with a variety of "educational" activities for their free time. Below are examples of activities my children were exposed to and explored at a young age. They spent every afternoon working on these skills, since TV and video games were off limits.

- By seventh grade, they became interested in building and programming LEGO Mindstorms robots.
- Website design is a great way to learn HTLM code. By sixth grade, they had their own page and spent hours coming up with new ideas.
- They took ice-skating and swimming lessons and also played soccer, basketball, tennis, and baseball.
- They enjoyed their private guitar lessons, but did not enjoy practicing every day. They were 7 years old when they started and after three years they took a break because they were not interested in practicing what they learned. A few years later, my older son asked for

an acoustic guitar for Christmas and now plays for fun daily. My younger son followed suit and even joined a band with friends. Although daily practice is linked to performance success, this activity should be fun. That's why constant nagging can result in children losing their passion for music. Musicians have inner pressure to improve their skill, and they practice because they enjoy it, not because they are forced into it. The focus should be on practicing quality and not quantity.

- They were allowed to watch movies and TV shows in Portuguese only. This helped them build vocabulary, learn Brazilian songs, and be exposed to another culture and customs.

- The Home Science Tools catalog offers everything a homeschooler may need for science projects. We purchased dissection/specimen kits, chemicals for projects, videos, and games.

- Educational games are available for every subject. Geography and World History games were our favorites. Games in a foreign language can be an interactive way to expand vocabulary.

- Building with LEGOS promotes fine motor skills, increases creativity, improves problem-solving skills, and helps develop persistence.

- By fifth grade, they were learning how to design video games using Scratch and Alice software. These online tools are free. (Start with Scratch; it's easier.)

- Spend time outdoors and enjoy nature. We would ride our bicycles to our neighborhood park a few times a week. Climb trees with your children and have a picnic on tree branches. We build relationships by interacting with others and children's connection with their parents is no different. This is a great way to build trust and show them the lighter side of you.

Since these activities were not structured, they could each explore their own passion. One of my sons is an avid reader; consequently, he read for hours every day while my elder son wrote a novel. They managed their own time and this skill helped them all the way through college.

Video games limit creativity and proper brain development; for that reason, limit children's game time. If they misbehaved, I would deduct 15 minutes of the allotted two hours for each incident. Withholding gaming time is an effective disciplinary tool.

NO MORE WHINING

My sons were not allowed to whine or say they were bored. If I heard them whining, I would ask them to repeat what they said in an acceptable tone of voice. If children develop a habit of talking back or whining, it can be difficult to stop.

Our household rules to stop whining:

First, define "whining" (asking for something repeatedly, begging, screaming, speaking in a high-pitched voice, making a sustained high-pitched crying sound). Print out 10 pages of math homework and put them in your purse. As soon as children complain of being bored, pull out a sheet and ask them to work out the problems. Don't make it fun. It should be boring. Even if they apologize and say that they will not do it again, they have to complete the assignment. I recommend this strategy for children over four.

Whining can become a bad habit and children use this tactic to annoy parents into submission. Have you ever talked to an adult who acts similar to a toddler? That's because whiny kids turn into whiny adults!

PUT AN END TO SIBLING FIGHTING

Sibling conflicts can be resolved without screaming or fighting over the perceived problem. It is crucial for children to understand how to handle conflicts at a young age, learn to apologize, and respect siblings and others equally. Respecting other people's points of view and acknowledging mistakes are essential skills. Some parents may say that it is normal for siblings to fight; I strongly disagree. We should respect our siblings, as we respect our friends.

Children can be taught to have self-control. How many people are harboring hurt feelings from interactions with siblings in their childhood? Unfortunately, I am one of those people and for that reason would not accept my sons mistreating and disrespecting each other. Managing conflicts and differences in a healthy, respectful manner wards off hurt feelings in the future. Even at a young age, discuss with your children how to alter the specific behavior that started the conflict.

My sons had friends over to our home a few times a week. They treated their friends with respect, shared their games, and learned to compromise. However, I noticed that sometimes my sons did not interact with each other respectfully. They would fight over everything and scream at each other frequently.

I had a plan to improve their relationship. I started to pay attention to how they treated their friends versus how they treated each other and jotted down some examples. I praised them on how they interacted with their friends, giving them examples of positive exchanges. I ignored their bickering with each other and concentrated on positive interactions with friends for a few months, hoping they would make the appropriate changes on their own.

Well, that did not happen, and I had to start giving them feedback about their relationship. For two months, I wrote down examples of interactions I did not approve of. My goal was for them to learn how to deal with their anger and find ways to resolve their differences, without fighting. They should feel comfortable to voice their concerns and work out conflicts and differences in opinion, in a respectful manner. I offered examples of positive and negative interactions they had with their friends and with each other, always stressing the positive interactions. Once we had these conversations, I warned them about possible repercussions if they chose not to treat each other with respect. I developed a rotation system where they took turns choosing a TV channel, which games to play, or which friends to have over; with the understanding that those activities were privileges and could be removed at any time if rules were not followed. I started with those activities, because they seemed to be the main source of disagreements.

Finally, I continued observing interactions they had with each other and friends always reminding them of the rules. I intervened if fights escalated; on the other hand, I let them deal with small confrontations. This is a long process, but if you're consistent and stick with it, it eventually pays off. After you do this for a few months, observe if your children are able to resolve confrontations by communicating and compromising. Allow them to work on their behavior for a month; however, continue to take notes on interactions with friends and siblings. Remind them of the rules for the first two weeks.

I was not happy with their progress; so I told them that if I caught them disrespecting each other, their friends would not be able to come to the house. Sadly, this went on for a few months before they finally began to treat each other respectfully. Mastering this skill helped them with future relationships with friends and co-workers. Children are bound to struggle with conflict throughout their lives; however, if they learn to respect differences in opinion, they will be more likely to resolve conflicts in a productive way.

SHOULD YOU BE YOUR CHILDREN'S REFEREE?

Parents have many jobs and responsibilities; however, being their children's referee and judge about who is right or wrong during sibling conflicts should not be one of them. Teach children to resolve problems on their own. However, if one child is being a bully, parents may have to intervene.

If other children are involved in the altercation, it is appropriate to speak to the parent rather than the child. Another adult should not confront or intimidate somebody else's child. Our job is to explain to the child's parents what happened and let them decide how to handle the situation. People handle situations differently, so if parents are not educating and teaching children to be respectful they may be a bad influence on your child anyway.

Although children are expected to be responsible, nice, and respectful, as parents, we should understand that they are people with different personalities and not little robots that can be programmed with sophisticated code. My two children have different personalities. An event that is extremely upsetting to one doesn't even faze the other. It is crucial to understand these traits and know that each child deals with issues differently.

It is important for children to learn to interact with one another, to deal with jealousy, to accept each other's personalities, assets, and flaws, and to mutually solve problems. It's all these combined experiences that prepare children for future relationships.

CHAPTER EIGHTEEN

BUILDING A POSITIVE RELATIONSHIP

AS CHILDREN GROW, THEY MAKE NEW FRIENDS, have new life experiences, and learn how to adhere to new rules. Parents also learn how to adjust their parenting approaches. Building a positive relationship with children creates trust and fosters open communication. Always be assertive and clear on your expectations.

Form a positive relationship with your children. Without being judgmental and breaking their trust, listen and help them to feel comfortable sharing their feelings. Although this can be difficult when you don't agree with their decisions, still share your thoughts and offer advice. As an example, my niece told a friend she no longer wanted to be friends because she did not like her personality. I had to explain to her that "personality" is a collection of traits and by describing her dislike as "personality," she simply told her friend that everything was wrong with her. We should be honest with people and give them constructive criticism that can help them and never hurt them.

Having special time with each child reaps a number of benefits. Your undivided attention helps a shy child get comfortable sharing feelings about topics he or she wouldn't share with the whole family. Try not to pry or ask for irrelevant details the child may be uncomfortable sharing.

Allow each child to pick a fun activity to do with you. If children receive the attention they crave, they will aspire to please you by making the right choices. Attention-seeking behavior, such as whining, is usually aggravated if a positive and healthy relationship is not present. My sons were accustomed to positive attention, but if they acted out in front of other people I would just give them the "disapproved look" and proceed to ignore them. That was enough to stop their undesirable behavior because it was perceived as a negative consequence.

Build a strong relationship and create great memories together by going camping, having dinner at a local restaurant, or just riding bikes.

DEALING WITH ANGER

Children's feelings of anger and jealousy need to be acknowledged. Parents should have a dialogue with each child to understand why he or she is upset.

My son would get sad whenever I called him out on his behavior; his facial expression and demeanor would change. It took me a while to understand that his reaction was aggravated by his fear that I would stop loving him if he did something wrong. I was unaware of this fear until I sat with him and told him that he was overreacting and I had to get his attention when he did something wrong. Once I told him my love was unconditional, he never reacted that way again.

Children need to learn how to interact with others and what behaviors are acceptable. Children get anxious when they're yelled at, so refrain from this behavior and use a softer voice to avoid sounding hostile.

WAYS TO COMMUNICATE AND PARENTING STYLE

Depending on their parenting style, parents have an impact on their children's development in a positive or negative way. Diana Baumrind, Ph.D., a clinical and developmental psychologist, identified four parenting styles: authoritarian, permissive, authoritative, and uninvolved.

Authoritarian parents refuse to empower children to be independent. They have firm rules and believe in punishment.

Permissive parents fail to teach children limits and self-control. They lack rules and discipline and are detached from their children's lives. With excessive freedom and minimum communication, this type of parenting is questionable.

Authoritative parents are willing to listen to questions. They set rules and expect them to be followed; however, they are more nurturing and forgiving rather than punishing.

Uninvolved parents offer little to no affection, security, or supervision, and they have few expectations. Neglectful parenting is often due to circumstances rather than choice.

Dr. Baumrind's research on parenting styles suggests, "Authoritative parents monitor and impart clear standards for children's conduct. They are assertive, yet not intrusive and restrictive. In addition, disciplinary methods are more supportive, rather than punitive. Their desire is for their children to be assertive in conjunction with socially responsible, and self-regulated in addition to cooperative."

Our goal should be to teach our children to deal with their emotions and have healthy relationships. Be a fair and respectful parent, who can be flexible at times. Reasonable rules and guidelines are essential, and children should be expected to follow them. When children are aware of consequences for breaking the rules, they are more likely to make the right decisions.

Should you be flexible? Although consistency is necessary, a little flexibility can be beneficial and offers children an incentive to work on new skills. I allowed my sons to earn extra video game time if they developed their own games. Gaming design is a valuable skill that helps develop problem-solving and critical-thinking skills.

Some parents authorize children to watch TV or play video games during the week, since it is convenient for them. The activities that my children were involved in required hours of my time to provide them with material and information to get them started. Once they got all the material and initial instructions, they independently finished their projects and followed directions, since clear expectations were set.

LEARN TO BE INDEPENDENT AND RESPONSIBLE

It is imperative for children to become independent and develop problem-solving skills at a young age. Responsibility and independence are skills that develop gradually and need to be adjusted as children grow. Kids can be exceedingly dependent on their parents and teachers and although this dependency is expected and acceptable during the first few years of elementary school, they eventually need to learn to take full responsibility for assignments, tests, and projects. Parents should have age-appropriate expectations, because responsibility and independence develop gradually. Problem-solving skills are essential and give children an edge not only in the school setting but also later in life.

Children should take responsibility for their schoolwork and projects. If they fail to complete assignments, they will learn that there are repercussions and hopefully refrain from repeating that mistake. This is the opportunity to have a discussion with them regarding responsibility, expectations, and possible consequences. Children, whose parents are controlling, do not take responsibility for their actions; while children, whose parents allow some freedom with defined boundaries, learn to be responsible and successful in school and later in life.

Allow children to exercise independence and maturity, and they will learn from their mistakes. Although we should check on children's progress on a daily basis, try not to be too obvious. The road to independence is rewarding for parents and children; on the other hand, if parents constantly make decisions for them, it affects their chance of becoming responsible and good citizens.

Although I was available if my children needed assistance, they knew that they had to take responsibility for their work. It is crucial that children take the initiative to complete their schoolwork on time. Resist the urge to help them with assignments and refrain from reminding them of due dates.

During a third grade parent-teacher conference, my son's teacher requested that I correct his homework before he turned it in to her. I questioned the reasoning behind that request and explained to her that students need to learn to take responsibility for their work; consequently, if I constantly check my son's work it would be counterproductive and deny him the opportunity to learn and grow. Undoubtedly, if parents check and help children with their work, they would get 100 percent on every assignment. As a result, they would not put the required effort into their work. On the hand, if the teacher grades according to the amount of effort put into their work, they would pay more attention in class and be more careful when answering questions.

If children make their own choices and take responsibility for their own work, they learn that for every bad choice there are consequences. Children, who have the freedom to make their own decisions, mature faster. Gradually expand their freedom.

Programs in the community can assist children in learning how to be good citizens. Boy Scout of America allows young adults to learn about teamwork, leadership, cooking, physical fitness, and community service. As of February of 2019, the organization elected to include girls into the program and changed its name to Scouts BSA.

Consider children's developmental stages when choosing the best discipline techniques.

WHAT TIME SHOULD CHILDREN GO TO BED?

Bedtime depends on age and should be altered for different phases of children's lives. Toddlers need to go to sleep at 7:30 p.m., and elementary school children can stay up an extra hour. My children earned 30 extra minutes every year after fifth grade. Remind younger siblings that when they get older, they will also have additional privileges. Judith Owens, M.D., director of the Pediatric Sleep Disorders Clinic at Hasbro Children's Hospital says, "The duration and the regularity of the sleep-wake cycle are the most important factors in a child's having a quality, restful sleep, and lack of sleep can have really devastating consequences on the child's mood and performance causing stress that stunts proper physical growth."

CARELESS ABOUT HOMEWORK

Students who attend conventional school are assigned homework daily. Homework reinforces what children learn at school, teaches perseverance, and time management. Although homework can bring some benefits, hours of daily homework is unnecessary.

Teachers do not have time to design thoughtful homework that would benefit each child, so they tend to assign busy work. I was so frustrated a few times when my elder son could not participate in his Cub Scout meetings or soccer practices because he had hours of homework. I took a close look at the homework and determined that it would not benefit him in any way. I contacted the teacher and her explanation was that she had to keep students busy at home. After I explained that my son was unable to participate in extracurricular activities and that most of the homework would not benefit him, she decided to assign less busy work. Some teachers may assign homework to complete content that is required to be taught before the mandatory annual assessment test. The No Child Left Behind Act put a lot of pressure on teachers who could not complete required lessons in class. Assigning those lessons as homework is common practice; however, it becomes overwhelming for students.

Homeschoolers, however, do not need homework to learn about perseverance and time management or to finish specific material. In addition, the one-to-one instruction allows them to reinforce and expand on material learned during school hours.

Parents who are supplementing their children's education at home can extract wrong answers from homework or tests to create lesson plans. This is a great way to eliminate gaps in your children's education.

Children should work on homework independently. Correct their work after they verified their answers a few times. If they got a math problem wrong, write it on a separate paper and ask them to solve the same problem one more time. If the answer is correct, identify why the mistake was made. Provide additional problems that require students to apply the concept learned. Occasionally, I found that homework errors were simply careless mistakes. One of my children was extremely inattentive and always in a hurry when checking his work. I stressed the importance of reviewing his schoolwork a few times and if he simply did not care and continued to make the same mistakes, there would be repercussions. However, consequences are only for children who are careless and not for those who don't understand the material.

This same method can be implemented to homeschooled children. If they do not understand a concept, prepare a lesson plan with multiple examples on the same idea used in the original problem. Follow the same method for English and other subjects. If students miss a comma or fail to capitalize a word, create a lesson plan that incorporates that rule. This repetition is guaranteed to work!

Elementary school years are an ideal time to learn about consequences, since grades are not as vital as they are in middle or high school.

IMPORTANCE OF CONSISTENCY

Consistency is essential when dealing with children. The way parents react to wrongdoing should be consistent to avoid confusion and anxiety.

My sons had a lot of homework when they were in elementary school, and it was important to have consistency in when they completed assignments to avoid an irreversible pattern of procrastination.

Children should understand what is expected of them and if their behavior warrants discipline, consequences should be feasible and not impact the entire family. Your tone has to match the severity of the conduct. Always have age-appropriate expectations and be consistent when disciplining children. Children's academic and social skills develop and improve when there is consistency and routine.

Should children be reminded of due dates?

The answer is simply NO. Assignments and test dates should be logged on their agenda, whether they are in a traditional school or homeschooled. Elementary school children, however, are unable to cope with complex time management skills; it is a learning process for them. The responsibility falls on parents at first, so assisting children log assignments on their agenda and teaching them time management skills early on helps avoid future problems. Children should work on mastering these skills while in elementary school, when grades are not as important.

Obviously, this is not the message parents should convey, but we all know elementary school grades won't affect their chances of getting into a top-rated high school or college. They eventually will take the initiative and responsibility to complete assignments and, in turn, improve their grades. Have my children ever forgotten to turn in an assignment and suffered consequences? Yes, countless times, and that was the best way for them to learn about responsibility and consequences. It only happened a few times before they realized that they had an aversion for failure.

POSITIVE AND NEGATIVE FEEDBACK

Constructive feedback encourages children to improve and should not impact their self-esteem. Feedback should be positive in tone and focus on a clear and achievable objective. The time and place to deliver criticism has to be appropriate, since it is difficult to accept any type of disapproval in front of others. The goal is to improve one's behavior, avoiding personal attacks.

Public and private school children are involved in posting viral shaming videos on Facebook and YouTube. Parents should warn children of how written statements posted on any kind of media can impact their future. An embarrassing picture or video can haunt them for a lifetime. When they apply for a job in the future, a mistake from the past could prevent them from landing the position.

Public humiliation, as a form of discipline, has been front and center in the news lately. In my opinion, shaming children or teenagers in public is an act of bullying. A father in Georgia put his daughter's furniture outside the house, because she did not clean her room. Another parent shot his daughter's laptop because of what she posted on Facebook. How about the parent who made his child hold a sign on the corner of a busy intersection with a list of behaviors he did not approve of? The choice to publicly ridicule children is disturbing; in addition, shaming them in public delivers the message that humiliation should be used as a deterrent.

Karyl McBride, Ph.D., a clinical psychologist based in Denver notes, "What they are modeling for their children is mean and cruel. Children learn more about what they see us do than anything we teach or preach to them."

Publicly shaming someone is not how people raise caring, empathetic, and secure children. The parent stops being the person who can dispense comfort and advice and turns into the one who betrayed them. Children should see parents as their allies and protectors. My mom never used humiliation as a tool and taught us to discern right from wrong.

In a perfect world, negative feedback should be interpreted as "retry" in a "different way," and a motivated student would perceive negative feedback as an incentive to improve himself and keep trying. Unfortunately, negative feedback can be traumatizing to students who feel they tried their best. The purpose of feedback is to improve performance, so offer them instantaneous feedback. I believe in positive feedback. That's why every time our children did something that went beyond what we expected of them, we would point it out to them. Although it is crucial to provide feedback while children are still mindful of the topic, negative feedback should be given in private.

- Take notice when children follow rules and acknowledge their effort. For example, "Dan, thanks for assisting your brother with math."
- Allow children to give feedback on your teaching techniques. If they feel it would benefit them to be taught in a different way, elaborate on the topic and apply some of their ideas. My sons provided me with feedback on my "failed" attempt to teach them how to dance. Although it seemed useful to me when they were able to dance at their first dance party.
- Offer children feedback while there is still time for them to correct their mistakes; however, be sure to take them aside to avoid embarrassment.

Positive feedback is critical. It sends people a signal that the behavior is correct and should be repeated.

The innocent permissiveness of today can be responsible for inadequate education in the future. A lenient parent makes few demands of their children and rarely disciplines them. Parents only realize they were permissive when their children are having behavior problems at school. Lack of discipline or boundaries at home affects them in school.

RULES AND EQUALITY

Although we let our children make their own decisions, we had plenty of rules to guide them. We created new rules, as needed. Explain the rules and the reasons to follow them. One of our rules was that our children had to treat each other with respect and fighting was not an option. It may seem impossible, but it works.

Allowing children to think for themselves does not imply consenting to let them do anything they want. While children should be treated equally and it is preferable not to show favoritism, if one child works harder and as a result obtains outstanding results academically, he or she should be rewarded.

This is yet another advantage of homeschooling. Parents can use that child as an example of what is expected of siblings. Of course, take into consideration that everyone is born with a specific talent and maybe one child is a math wiz and the other is great in history. In that case, maybe they can work together to achieve the best results.

In the school system, students who excel academically are simply ignored since teachers are too busy dealing with children who are misbehaving or academically challenged. Although schools are not allowed to compare students, they are constantly being compared with one another and teachers expect them to excel at the same pace, which is unrealistic.

CHAPTER NINETEEN

HONOR SOCIETIES

HONOR SOCIETY ORGANIZATIONS PROVIDE like-minded students with opportunities to earn community service hours, provide extracurricular activities, scholarship opportunities, and social events.

National Honor Society

Being a member of the National Honor Society is very commendable, since only students who demonstrate high academic achievement are invited to participate. Members have an advantage of getting scholarships for college. To join the NHS, students must be enrolled at a school with an active NHS chapter. The minimum requirements, per the NHS National Constitution, are the following:

- Maintaining a cumulative grade point average of 3.0 (unweighted).
- Being involved in volunteering or service hours.
- Maintaining good behavior.
- Participating in leadership roles.

Homeschoolers are not allowed to join the National Honor Society; however, the organizations below provide equal opportunities for homeschoolers.

Eta Sigma Alpha National Homeschool Honor Society

Eta Sigma Alpha National Homeschool Honor Society recognizes homeschool students and provides scholarships. Students, grades nine to 12, who have scored 1200 on the SAT or PSAT, are eligible to join the chapter in their state or the national chapter. In addition, homeschoolers must have a 3.5 GPA, be homeschooled a minimum of 50 percent of the time, and meet the HSLDA definition of a homeschooler.

Mu Eta Sigma National Math Honor Society

Mu Eta homeschool honor society was founded to encourage students with strong math skills.

Science National Honor Society

With all the scientific advancement, recognizing high school students in the sciences is imperative. The Science National Honor Society is a scientific organization that recognizes young scientists who will be the future of industry, research, and scientific discoveries.

CHAPTER TWENTY

DEVELOPMENTAL STAGES

IT IS EXTREMELY BENEFICIAL FOR PARENTS to understand Jean Piaget's Four Stages of Cognitive Development. Jean Piaget, Ph.D., was highly influential in the areas of development and psychology, believing that children constructed their own knowledge. His philosophy is the foundation for the "constructivist" theory, which states that learners are more likely to be engaged in learning when it is relevant and meaningful. Dr. Piaget identified four stages every child passes through. It is crucial to understand these stages when homeschooling because this knowledge helps parents choose the best material for each stage. Keep in mind, however, that most of Piaget's work describes the typical child and does not take into account bi- or multilingualism, heredity, and culture. His theory can be used as a guideline and adjusted to the uniqueness of each child.

SENSORIMOTOR STAGE (BIRTH TO 24 MONTHS)

Use of motor activity: This is the stage where infants discover the relationship between bodies and environment. They discover the concept of object permanence, where the object is present even if removed from the visual field.

Limited knowledge: Two processes are responsible for how children acquire and use new information.

- **Assimilation:** Is the cognitive process where children incorporate new information into existing knowledge base. This concept does not only apply to children, adults also encounter new ideas daily and make adjustments to existing ideas.

- **Accommodation:** When children adjust to new information. Old ideas are replaced based on new information.

Memory is developing (object permanence): One illustration of this stage is when children conceal their eyes and believe that adults cannot see them. My sons would jump on my husband's back and think that they were invisible. In this stage, they learn that even if they cannot see an object or person it continues to exist.

Environmental and sociocultural differences

Language development starts during the sensorimotor phase. This is the stage where children can represent ideas via language; however, it does not address environment aspects such as learning a foreign language and other sociocultural influences that affect a child's development. Again, Piaget's work describes a typical child and does not take into account delays based on a child learning a second language, which was my son's case.

Concerned about my son's speech delay, I took him to the doctor for a hearing checkup and results showed no impairment. Looking back, however, I could have helped my son speak sooner. Every time I would ask my son a question, his elder brother would reply for him; consequently, he did not feel the need to respond. Today, I understand that giving him a toy without him using his words only fueled the issue. This delay, fortunately, did not cause future problems, and he ended up being a straight-A student all the way through college.

PRE-OPERATIONAL STAGE (2 TO 7 YEARS OF AGE)

- Improved communication skills.
- Improved memory.
- Cause and effect.

Imagination is developed at this stage, along with memory. My younger son was my joyful child. He pranced around the house dressed up with different Halloween outfits and masks always trying to scare the family. This stage is when children engage in make-believe. His favorite costume was of Spider-Man, and he would not remove the outfit and mask for anything. Kids at this stage tend to be egocentric and have a difficult time understanding other people's perspectives. They are unable to conceptualize that someone else's point of view could differ from theirs. For example, "if my favorite food is pizza, my friend's favorite food must be pizza too!"

CONCRETE OPERATIONAL STAGE (7 TO 11 YEARS OLD)

- Aware of environment.
- Think logically: Children at this stage start to think logically and understand the principles of cause and effect. At this stage, children are no longer egocentric and understand that other people have different viewpoints.

FORMAL OPERATIONAL STAGE (11 YEARS AND UP)

- Ability to think abstractly: Although Dr. Piaget talks about stages that define specific ages, we all know that changes do not happen in a linear manner. There are also environmental factors to be considered. Some people may exhibit patterns from the last stage and not have the ability to think about abstract concepts all the time.
- Shows interest in social, political, and ethical issues.
- Abstract and systematic thinking at this stage is similar to an adult.

Activities that deviate from Piaget's theory

Piaget's theory stresses that the content of instruction needs to be in line with the developmental stages of the student. Our role, as teachers, is to provide a range of experiences and encourage learning. The use of concrete hands-on material and visual aids facilitates the learning experience. As an example, we used stories and cartoons to learn and associate multiplication facts with the characters of the story.

Although Piaget's theory suggests that teaching children developmentally advanced material would be ineffective, from our experience this theory did not hold true. Developmentally appropriate practice is the process of deciding what is best and most appropriate for children, based on their individual age and stage of development. This includes discipline, food, scheduling, and communication.

From my experience, children are capable of learning advanced concepts at an early age and although it is vital to select content that matches the cognitive capacities of students, undoubtedly students can benefit from more in-depth material. My sons were taking high school classes starting in sixth grade. By the time my son went to high school, he had taken many high school honors classes (Algebra I, Algebra II, World History, Physical Science, Geometry, and American History). We had to obtain special permission for one of my sons to sign up for an 11th grade American History honors class, since he was still in seventh grade. Both of my sons earned an A in every upper-level class they took.

Since my children were homeschooled, I made sure that they were exactly at the level that they were capable of and not where the school system dictated they should be.

My sons learned science and math through active involvement with the environment and through correlation with the real world. We spent every summer in North Carolina and looked forward to exploring the creeks and woods. They observed and caught frogs, snakes, humming birds, turtles, and any bug that crossed their path. With no Internet or cable at our cabin, my children had plenty of time to enjoy the outdoors. They kept the insects for a few days while they researched their origin, species, food they ate, and eventually released them. I know, you're probably wondering how did they catch a humming bird? They are so fast. My older son was extremely patient and spent hours observing them and waited for the right opportunity to catch one. The main goal was not to harm the bird and he released him after a few minutes. He only kept the bat for one night after finding out that bats eat thousands of bugs a day and realizing it would not be an easy task feeding the bat. Today, there are apps that help identify insects.

Offer children context that is developmentally appropriate and sequentially increased in depth as they advance through school. Have discussions with them about social and cultural issues, ensuring that the context is meaningful and relevant to them.

We watched the world news daily. Topics were selected based on issues I wanted to discuss with my children. Since I recorded the news using a DVR, I was able to censor topics that were too weighty. We would have discussions on topics related to our state, the nation, and the world. We observed contradictory points of view from reporters of different networks. By the time they were 12 years old, they were able to follow every political and social issue. This was history in the making, and I felt that my children were mature enough to understand the topics and have their own opinions. They were able to discern the party affiliation of reporters, just by listening to them. Have a discussion with your children and explain how the news can be distorted, depending on what station is reporting it. Newspapers and magazines from different countries offer different points of view and it became a game trying to figure out whether a network sided with the Democrats or Republicans.

Listening to one source of news can be deceptive; consequently, the only way to acquire a glimpse of the truth is by listening to a variety of news channels and reading different newspapers. Much of the media is not interested in informing, but rather guiding viewers to their opinion. Although viewers expect TV news to be unbiased, allowing the listener to make educated decisions, the fact is that it is an environment of judgment and attack. Learning should be enjoyable and challenging.

INTERACTING WITH CHILDREN

At school, children fail to ask questions due to pressure or fear of being wrong or ridiculed. Also, there isn't enough time for 20 children to ask all the questions they have. How can anyone learn if they can't ask questions? Children who are homeschooled are free to roam and explore unique possibilities by asking questions and researching topics of interest. Due to the flexibility of homeschooling, we do not stop at answering that "one" question. We expand on the topic and even make it into a lesson plan.

Show interest in your children's daily activities by starting a conversation about what happened that day. This gives them a chance to share any issues or concerns they may have. My elder son was talkative and shared every detail of his day. However, my younger son, always extremely quiet, had difficulty starting a conversation. I remember one day asking him what happened at school that day and he had nothing to say. He said, "Mom, what do people talk about?" "Anything that happened at school, interactions with friends, or you can just ask questions," I replied. An hour later, he says. "I won the spelling bee at school today, which means I get to represent the entire school at the Broward County Convention Center." I could not believe that he had won the spelling bee for the entire school, including fifth graders (he was a fourth grader). He did not consider this a big deal and it did not even occur to him to share this tremendous accomplishment. He had the tendency to communicate using one-word answers and did not elaborate on a topic. I realized it was vital for me to work with him until he was able to have full conversations with the family.

HOW IS BACKGROUND NOISE LINKED TO CONCENTRATION?

Eliminate distractions is the typical advice offered to students to improve study habits. Is this good advice? Some people work better with background noise. My older son and I need background noise to concentrate, while my younger son and husband can only function in a silent room.

Research done by psychologist Russell Green demystifies the reasoning behind this. Dr. Green gave math problems to introverts and extroverts, using varying levels of background noise. He found that the extroverts performed better with higher noise levels and the introverts with lower noise levels. He claims that introverts and extroverts operate in different levels of stimulation.

IS YOUR CHILD AN INTROVERT OR EXTROVERT?

An introvert prefers a quiet and low-key environment, while an extrovert needs more stimulation. An introverted person is not necessarily antisocial; they just prefer to socialize in a quieter way.

It is important to identify whether your children are introverts or extroverts because that determines what type of environment would better suit them. Keep in mind, however, that most workplaces are designed for extroverts. Most offices have open floor plans and no walls to separate desks, which is a distracting environment for introverts. The noise level in an open office plan can even make it difficult for extroverts to concentrate.

Respect your children's preference for silence whenever possible, but realize that can be an unrealistic expectation most of the time.

MAKING EXCUSES FOR CHILDREN

"My son is smart, but he does not do well in school because he is bored…"

How many times have you heard parents make this comment? There are many reasons for students to feel bored at school. They may not be sufficiently challenged, the teaching method used is not individualized, having to wait until everyone finishes their work is frustrating, teaching material already mastered, or students may be unmotivated. Parents should identify the issue and find the solution to help their children excel academically. Boredom should never be used as an excuse to not succeed in school.

A combination of factors caused my sons not to like school. Having to wait for other students to finish their work, teachers repeating material year after year, and not learning enough were some of the reasons. Regardless of all these issues, they both kept an A average.

Parents who use the excuse that gifted children are not doing well in school because they are bored are granting these children permission to not apply themselves or work harder. Sometimes students say they are bored because they are having difficulty learning and not necessarily because school is too easy for them.

Complaining about being bored is an ongoing problem in the school system and can lead to bigger issues such as bullying, fights, and depression. This is not the school or teacher's responsibility. Parents need to intervene, identify the problem, and either resolve the situation themselves or work with the teacher to address the issue.

My children had difficulties with certain subjects in school; consequently, I knew that I needed to provide them with the necessary tools to improve their understanding of those topics to ensure they did not fall behind.

At the same time, my elder son complained that school was too easy and he was not learning enough. Since he got straight A's and did well on standardized tests, I knew school was too easy. Listen to your children and act accordingly. After meeting with his teacher, she signed him up for a higher-level online math program; however, he still had to attend the "easy" math class and do the extra work during recess. Obviously, her approach was not successful, because he preferred to socialize with friends, rather than learn more advanced math.

Refrain from allowing children to use laziness or boredom as an excuse not to succeed in school. This is a disservice to them! Link intelligence with how well they perform at school. They should learn from their mistakes and strive to do better.

IS THE STUDENT UNDERPERFORMING DUE TO ANXIETY?

Everyone gets nervous before a test; however, test anxiety can be debilitating to some students. Physical symptoms such as a headache and fast heartbeat can be an issue before taking an exam. The Anxiety and Depression Association of America (ADAA), an international organization, offers tips on how to overcome anxiety. Below are tips from the ADAA and Mental Health America (MHA) on how to deal with stress:

- Put your stress in perspective.
- Do your best. Do not aim for perfection.
- Have a positive attitude.
- Find out what triggers your anxiety.
- Avoid caffeine because it aggravates anxiety.
- Eat balanced meals.
- Sleep eight hours a night. (Teenagers need to sleep more.)
- Exercise.
- Take deep breaths when stressed.
- Count slowly to 10.

Regardless of whether children underperform due to lack of interest or anxiety, it is our obligation to help them solve the problem.

NEVER GIVE UP

I always taught my children that they should never quit. I emigrated to this country without speaking a word of English and managed to earn an electrical engineer degree. I spent numerous nights awake, so that I could translate six chapters worth of material to study for a test. Overcoming challenges by putting extra effort into a difficult situation is a critical skill to teach children.

Math is a continuous learning experience. If children work through difficulties they encounter in math, they will learn to work through other issues they face in life. Having an "I will not give up" mindset teaches children to be persistent until they achieve their goal.

INJUSTICE CAN GET IN THE WAY OF COMPASSION

My boys would often come home from school frustrated because the teacher cancelled recess because one child misbehaved. Punishing the entire class for the misconduct of one student is common practice in the school system. Some teachers would force everyone to run a lap with no explanation of why they were being punished. Later, they would find out that they were again being punished for the wrongdoing of one student. This happens so often that school children grow immune to this situation and believe that this is the way it has to be. Teachers believe that peer pressure from the children who were unjustly punished encourages the misbehaving child to modify his or her behavior and, in return, the teacher will regain control of the classroom. That is nonsense!

Having worked for large corporations such as Motorola and Allied Signal for decades, I have never been in a similar situation. Engineers were individually rated and ranked based on their performances. There were a number of engineers responsible for an individual project and the members of each small group would take responsibility for their section. If part of the cell phone or radar system did not work, the manager would not blame every engineer on the project and require everyone to work late to fix the problem. The same occurs at the university level. If one student breaks the rules and uses a cell phone during class, interrupting the lecture, the professor does not punish everyone.

In my opinion, the way misbehavior is handled in the school system is unacceptable and ineffective. Children become numbed by the inherent injustice of group punishment. This only teaches them that nobody will ever take responsibility for his or her own actions, which is unrealistic.

Homeschooling means that parents can provide grounds for justice and never punish all the children because of one child's misbehavior. There is an exception for this. If my children fought over a toy or game and it escalated to a point where it was unacceptable, I would hold them both responsible. I felt that they should have self-control and if they were not able to talk to each other and work out issues in a civil manner, both had failed. After a few times of removing their game, they learned to communicate with each other and not escalate the argument to the point where I would have to intervene.

Children and adults should be compassionate and kind. If children and adults are surrounded by injustice, they tend to lose their sense of compassion.

Eventually students from my sons' school found out which student was responsible for making them miss recess and the entire class turned against that child. Without realizing it, the teacher gave that child the desired attention he wanted and thus reinforced the unacceptable behavior. I explained to my sons that although I did not agree with the way the teacher took control over the situation, they should sympathize with the child who caused the problem. They were flabbergasted and shouted. "What? I do not like that kid."

I explained that perhaps that child could be having problems at home, which caused him to act that way. I knew there were children in the class who were homeless or were foster children and told them that we are not aware of the difficulties they were facing. After explaining why some children are homeless, they were able to understand my point of view.

To ensure that they had a wider view of society and not become complacent in their perfect, secure world, we teamed up with a neighbor and made necessity bags for the homeless at the local shelter. We visited the shelter and sadly observed children piled up on bunk beds with hardly any room to move. I explained to my sons that these children also attend school and emphasized how difficult it must be to complete assignments in such a noisy environment.

The lesson here was to teach my sons about empathy and compassion for others. After this experience, my children became more understanding and could put things into prospective.

CHAPTER TWENTY-ONE

BE PREPARED FOR UNFORESEEN CIRCUMSTANCES

LIFE THROWS CURVE BALLS AT US SOMETIMES. Unexpected events can bring serious consequences. Homeschool parents may wish that nothing will ever change and that their children will never have to go back to public school. However, plans can change and sometimes we may have no control over them. Nobody is exempt from unexpected events, so children should be academically prepared to reduce stress.

A CAR ACCIDENT CHANGED MY PLANS

I was in a terrible car accident, while still homeschooling my younger son. I picked my sons up from soccer practice and as we sat at a red light, a drunk driver hit my car and four others at 60 miles an hour. Luckily, nothing happened to my children, but I spent the next two years in excruciating pain and had to have a three-level cervical surgery. Today, I am fully recovered. This unfortunate event made it difficult to continue homeschooling my younger son, because I was also diagnosed with occipital neuralgia. My eyes were blurry most of the day, and I was bedridden for almost two years before and after surgery.

My elder son had already entered a local program where he would earn his high school and college degree at the same time. He was only 14, so I was still responsible for getting him to school. I am glad I had been proactive in ensuring that my children were advanced academically with no gaps in their education, because my son had to return to a brick-and-mortar school after the accident.

Life can change in the blink of an eye. One day I was this healthy homeschool mom who was busy teaching, taking my sons on field trips, travelling all over the country when suddenly everything changed. As a previously active person, being bedridden was devastating.

My husband gave me the idea to write about our successful homeschool journey. Even though I was unable to see clearly, I could type. Writing this book and having the desire to share my experience with other homeschoolers took my mind off my chronic pain and inability to walk.

The techniques in this book provide the tools needed to build a solid education that is aligned with accepted standards and free of gaps that could prove problematic if homeschoolers have to reenter the school system due to unforeseen circumstances.

By the end of that year, my son took the entrance exam test for Florida Atlantic University. The admission to this program is merit based. So, besides passing the entrance exam, he had to prove that he was mature enough to handle college classes at 14. Out of the thousands who apply only 100 get accepted. Luckily, he got accepted. Students complete ninth grade at the high school and can earn up to 15 university credits that year.

CHAPTER TWENTY-TWO

FROM HOMESCHOOL TO HARVARD

A LOT OF PARENTS HAVE ASPIRATIONS for their children to get into an Ivy League school, preferably Harvard. I must confess that I did not have that dream. When my son was ready to apply for a research program after earning his bachelor's degree, he decided to apply to a few Ivy League schools. He was thrilled when he got an interview with University of Pennsylvania and Harvard and got accepted into both programs. He declined the interview request from University of Chicago and other universities after being accepted into Harvard.

He was offered a stipend to conduct research in the field of neuroscience at both universities. He accepted Harvard's offer, which included a $35,000 stipend, moving expenses, free upper graduate classes, and medical insurance.

HOMESCHOOLERS' EXPERIENCES AT HARVARD

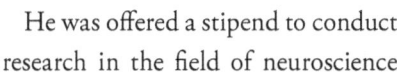

Below you will find information about my son's program and an article based on interviews with homeschoolers who got accepted into Harvard.

The Research Scholar Initiative is a post-baccalaureate program that allows students to perform research with a Harvard faculty member as a research assistant. In addition to performing neuroscience research, my son took graduate- level classes in preparation for his doctoral degree. Harvard accepts economics and life sciences students as well. Students can live in the dorm or rent an apartment in Boston. The problem with the dorm is that it is located in Cambridge and most of the neuroscience research is done at the medical school in Longwood. Since my son had to be at the medical school every morning, he decided to live in Austin.

Sofia W. Tong and Idil Tuysuzoglu wrote an article in The Harvard Crimson about homeschoolers who got admitted into Harvard.

Here is a summary of the article. (The full article can be found online.)

- Harvard Admission Office's Website: "Each applicant to Harvard College is considered with great care and homeschooled applicants are treated the same as all other applicants."
- Dean of Freshmen Thomas A. Dingman says, "Homeschoolers integrate well into the student population. We've had lots of success with students who identify as homeschooled."
- Sukumar, a student who was homeschooled up to the ninth grade, said that homeschool was helpful in shaping her attitude towards schooling. "Generally, I feel less burned out than other people do. I never felt the need to get time off or to adapt here."
- Farrar, a student who was homeschooled until college, says that the common misconception that homeschoolers are socially inept is far from the truth.

Although Harvard does not offer statistics on how many homeschooled applicants are accepted, they claim that the admissions office evaluates traditional school students and homeschooled applicants the same way.

My elder son is now 21 years old and finishing his post-baccalaureate program at Harvard. He applied for a neuroscience Ph.D. program and got accepted into Harvard, Yale, Johns Hopkins, Princeton, UCSF, University of Chicago, Mt. Sinai, and Stanford. He decided to accept Stanford's offer because he wanted to transition into the technology side of neuroscience and Harvard's concentration is more in biological research.

IMPORTANT TIPS

- If graduate school is not part of your plan, a bachelor's degree from a top-rated university is important. However, if students are planning on earning a master's degree or getting into a Ph.D. program, spending a substantial amount of money on an Ivy League school for an undergraduate degree is unnecessary.
- Do students need a master's degree before applying for a Ph.D. program? Most universities do not require a master's degree, so students can apply right after their bachelor's program.
- By going straight into a Ph.D. program, students are offered a stipend to cover living expenses. All classes are free, since students work as a research or teacher's assistant.
- Not all universities require the GRE test.
- Undergraduate students can apply for a job at the university as early as their first year. My elder son applied for a TA position to teach biology.

Although most teaching assistant jobs are offered to graduate students, both undergraduate and graduate students could apply for this position.

Biology lecture classes had about 300 students and discussion classes had 20 to 30 students. The university's professor taught the main class and the teaching assistant ran the discussion class. Since the lecture classes were so large and the professors could not answer everyone's questions, the university created discussion classes.

My younger son took a position tutoring math at the university's Mathematics Learning Center. Students can also work at the library or food court, although a teaching assistant position looks better on a resume.

Is graduate school necessary? You may not get noticed with an undergraduate degree because more highly qualified candidates may be applying for the same positions. Graduate students pursue their interest more in-depth, which enables them to become experts in their specific area of study. Most corporations require a master's degree.

Twenty years ago, students with a bachelor's degree in engineering could get a good job easily and a master's degree was optional. Today, engineers with a bachelor's degree can still find a job, but at much lower salaries and diminished promotion opportunities. Most of the open positions require a master's degree or someone with a bachelor's degree and a minimum of 10 years' experience. My younger son earned his Bachelor's degree in Electrical Engineering at age of 19 and found a job with a small start-up right out of school. Although one viable path would be to continue forward gaining training and experience in the workforce, my son realized that an advanced degree would better position him to succeed in the long term. He applied to Georgia Tech's engineering PhD program and was accepted and offered a full ride covering tuition and living expenses. For someone with a business degree, which is a competitive field, not having a master's degree from a reputable university could be an issue.

CHAPTER TWENTY-THREE

CONCLUSION

HOMESCHOOLERS ARE MOTIVATED BY A VARIETY of factors, including philosophical, political, religious, school violence, future pandemics, or simply a better academic solution. The fact is that whatever the reason, the motive is always the same: All homeschool parents decide to take a stand and find an enhanced way to educate their children.

There is no right or wrong way to homeschool. While some families rely on educational programs and videos, others prefer not to own a television set. Some are highly regimented and have a set schedule and tests, others work whenever time allows. Many parents use outside sources to teach their children, while others teach all the subjects themselves.

The sad truth is that most children are not fortunate enough to have such an opportunity. Perhaps the family needs the second income or feels inept when it comes to teaching. If the reason is the latter, I must say that anyone can homeschool his or her children. There is plenty of assistance out there; homeschool parents are not alone. There is no need for parents to excel in every subject their children will study. They just need to have the willingness to be involved and learn along with them.

Being able to provide each child with one-on-one attention, offering wholesome and engaging social opportunities, and assisting with difficult concepts are gifts parents can provide to their children.

If not having time to teach is a recurring event, perhaps it is time to put them back in school. It is not fair to children if life is too hectic and homeschooling is not a priority. They need to make progress and learn as much as they can. Homeschooling can be demanding and it is not for everyone. If the parent is unprepared or reluctant to make this important commitment, there are other options.

Parents have different concerns on whether to homeschool their children or not. They may believe that they are not patient, socialized, educated, or organized enough to teach. Believe me, whatever you consider your shortcomings to be, they can and will improve as you homeschool.

As for socialization, no parent's desire is to raise socially inept children. Once you join a homeschool group, you'll find there are plenty of opportunities to socialize. Some homeschool parents put socialization ahead of academics and choose to socialize on a daily basis, leaving academic work to be done in the car between events. Ultimately, they always find time for academics, and their children always score high on standardized tests.

If parents feel they are not qualified to homeschool their children, remember children are extremely independent and can learn a great deal on their own. For those subjects that are challenging, online classes are available and can help alleviate stress. Some are free of charge and children have a full-time teacher available to answer questions at any time of the day.

As a substitute teacher for the public schools and after volunteering in the public-school system, I must say that even teachers doubt themselves. I recall being a volunteer in a science class and after the teacher gave a lecture on mass, she kept using the term weight and mass interchangeably. The fact is that mass is not the same as weight. This happened more times than I was comfortable admitting. Answers are not readily available to teachers while the material is being taught. At home, parents can search for answers online.

If homeschool parents feel they are not patient or organized enough, maybe this is a good opportunity to change. Children model their parent's positive and negative traits, so this might be a good time for parents to reevaluate and work on these characteristics themselves. Another advantage of homeschooling is the ability to travel without the constraint of school calendar.

Although there may be other benefits and disadvantages related with homeschooling, I am confident the information in this book provides parents with the tools they need to become successful homeschool parents.

BIBLIOGRAPHY

ADAA. "Home." *Anxiety and Depression Association of America, ADAA*, adaa.org/."Fixed Mindset vs. Growth Mindset (What Characteristics Are Critical to Success)." Develop Good Habits, 24 Apr. 2019, www.developgoodhabits.com/fixed-mindset-vs-growth-mindset/.

Dweck, Carol S. *Mindset: The New Psychology of Success*. New York: Random House, 2006. Print.

Dweck, Carol S. Carol Dweck's *Mindset: The New Psychology of Success: Summary*. Ant Hive Media, 2016.

Frank, Christina. "5 Teen Behavior Problems: A Troubleshooting Guide." *WebMD,* WebMD, www.webmd.com/parenting/features/behavior-problems#1.

Homeschool Legal Defense Association. "Homeschooling Advocates since 1983." *HSLDA*, hslda.org/content.

"Jean Piaget." *Criticism* -. Web. 09 Jan. 2016. <http://piaget.weebly.com/criticism.html>.

Kendrick Williams. "*The Quietest People Have the Loudest Thoughts: Introversion in Society*." MOSAIC Cross-Cultural Center, 21 Feb. 2017, mosaicsjsu.wordpress.com/2017/02/21/the-quietest-people-have-the-loudest-thoughts-introversion-in-society-kendrick-williams/.

Kimball, Miles. "*How to Turn Every Child into a 'Math Person.'*" Quartz, Quartz, 11 Aug. 2014, qz.com/245054/how-to-turn-every-child-into-a-math-person/.

Lieszkovszky, Ida. "*My toddler is a night owl: Multitasking Moms and Dads.*" Cleveland.com. 23 Sept. 2018. Cleveland.com. 04 June 2019. <https://www.cleveland.com/parents/2018/09/my_toddler_is_a_night_owl_mult.html>.

National Archives. "From 1900 to 2000." *The Cabinet Papers*, The National Archives, Kew, Surrey TW9 4DU, 5 Jan. 2009, www.nationalarchives.gov.uk/cabinetpapers/maps-in-time.htm.

National Center for Education Statistics (NCES) Home Page, Part of the U.S. Department of Education." *National Center for Education Statistics* (NCES) Home Page, a Part of the U.S. Department of Education, nces.ed.gov/.

Nisbett, Richard E. *Intelligence and How to Get It: Why Schools and Cultures Count.* New York: W.W. Norton, 2009/2010.

Pruett.Brown, Kyle and Laura Lewis. "The Benefits of Music Education." PBS. PBS. Web. 08 Jan. 2016. <http://www.pbs.org/parents/education/music-arts/the-benefits-of-music-education/>.

Psychology Today. *"Musical Training Optimizes Brain Function." Psychology Today,* Sussex Publishers, www.psychologytoday.com/us/blog/the-athletes-way/201311/musical-training-optimizes-brain-function.

Sabbagh, Leslie. "*The Teen Brain, Hard at Work.*" Scientific American. June 2007.

Science Daily. "*Musical training shapes brain anatomy, affects function.*" *Science Daily.* 12 Nov. 2013. ScienceDaily. 04 June 2019 <https://www.sciencedaily.com/releases/2013/11/131112163216.htm>.

Sooriya, P. *Parenting Style.* Ashok Yakkaldevi, 2017.

2007 National Institutes of Health Public Access twin study.

Tong, Sofia W, and Idil Tuysuzoglu. "*From Homeschool to Harvard: News: The Harvard Crimson.*" News | The Harvard Crimson,Dec. 10th, 2017, www.thecrimson.com/article/2017/12/10/homeschool-harvard/.

Wanjek, CM. "*Learning a New Language at Any Age Helps the Brain.*" LiveScience. 02 June 2014. Purch. 04 June 2019 <https://www.livescience.com/46048-learning-new-language-brain.html>.

"How to turn every child into a "math person" — Quartz." Quartz — Global business news and insights. Web. <http://qz.com/245054/how-to-turn-every-child-into-a-math-person/>.

"40 Tweets from Parents about Homeschooling amid COVID-19 | HuffPost Life." HuffPost - Breaking News, U.S. and World News | HuffPost. Web. <http://www.huffpost.com/entry/tweets-parents-homeschool-kids-coronavirus_l_5e836732c5b6d38d98a5976e>.

APPENDIX A

Article written by Florida Atlantic University Research Division (CM is my elder son and DM my younger son)

HOME-GROWN SKILLS SPUR NEUROSCIENCE RESEARCH

CM's undergraduate research may help scientists combat Huntington's disease, a devastating neurological disorder that results in progressive loss of speech, thinking, reasoning, and motor coordination.

He worked under the supervision of Jianning Wei, Ph.D., associate professor in the Biomedical Sciences Department, investigating one of the possible underlying mechanisms of the disease. In normal brain cells, tiny structures called lysosomes digest worn-out particles throughout the cell. In Huntington's disease, the lysosomes clump together, indicative of functional defects. It is an inherited disorder caused by a faulty gene that manufactures a mutant, overly sticky protein. Wei's lab studies the role the mutant protein plays in clumping the lysosomes together.

Using the CRISPR-Cas9 gene-editing tool, CM developed a line of cells that lacked the gene altogether. He then used a special microscope that produces high-resolution photographs to compare these cells against those that occur in nature. His findings backed Wei's hypothesis that the mutant protein, called huntingtin, contributes to the abnormal clumping.

"CM worked as an independent researcher under my supervision," said Wei. "He conducted the experiment, analyzed the data and presented the work at an undergraduate symposium. This novel cellular model should help us better understand the function of huntingtin in protein trafficking."

CM might have used sophisticated equipment at FAU, but the fundamental tools behind his research lay at home. When he and his brother, DM, were in elementary school, their mother left her engineering job at Motorola to home-school them. It was the most difficult decision Eloisa Minasi had ever made, but it paid off when both boys got into FAU High School — a public school that transitions rising sophomores to the University for three years of undergraduate study. There, CM and DM earned 3.9-plus averages and won FAU's Presidential Award. DM, who is 17 years old, is currently in his third year in electrical engineering, and CM recently received his BA in neuroscience at the age of 18.

CM is well aware of the benefits his mother's tutelage gave him. "Homeschooling definitely had an effect on my attitudes and work habits," he said. "My mother was very thorough in creating a personalized and well-rounded curriculum for me. She also pushed me to develop one very important skill: the capacity to self-learn. That was the single most important ability I used to succeed in college."

Now CM is heading to Harvard, where he plans on earning a Ph.D. in neuroscience. He's received a $35,000 research stipend, a relocation package and will take graduate courses at no cost.

And Eloisa? The FAU alumna is back in the engineering field, designing communications systems for the Department of Defense. Her husband, also an engineer, designs Lidar systems for self-driving cars. Both happily give professional advice to students who are interested in engineering, although Eloisa has taken down her home-schooling shingle.

APPENDIX B

HOMESCHOOL CURRICULUM SURVEY

Are you curious about what curriculums other homeschool parents are using? I have surveyed thousands of homeschoolers throughout the United States and compiled a list of their favorite curriculums. A lot of the options are FREE. A more comprehensive list will be on my website www.fromhomeschooltoharvard.com

All subjects

- Easy Peasy (Free)
- Core Knowledge (Free K-8th) *
- CK12 (Free K-college)
- IXL (Free and paid) *
- Freedom Homeschooling (Free)

> "My favorite curriculum is Gather Round homeschool. It is a unit study using Charlotte Mason approach, which allows me to teach all of my children (pre-K, K, 2nd and 4th grades) together. I love that it has book recommendations by level to go deeper into the topics covered.
>
> We have also utilized resources from freedomhomeschooling.com. We LOVE Easy Peasy as a free option and still use some of their stuff even though we do Gather Round mostly now."
>
> **Christy Clontz**
>
> *Homeschool parent from Indiana Author of*
> "The homeschooling mom.org".

History

- Good and the Beautiful (Free courses)
- Story of the World *
- Notgrass
- Beautiful Feet
- Lifepac

Language Arts

- The Good and the Beautiful
- IEW *
- Memoria Press
- All about Reading
- Brave Writer

> "www.schoolhouseteachers.com is the curriculum wing of The Old Schoolhouse Magazine (TOSMagazine.com). I think you will be amazed to see all they offer! The Old Schoolhouse Magazine is the Trade magazine for Homeschooling anywhere and everywhere. They provide a free digital copy with so much information - quarterly - it is amazing! Print subscriptions are also available."
>
> **Rita Chamberlin**
> *Certified Teacher*

Math

- Khan Academy (Free)
- Master Books
- Beast Academy (Grades 2-5)
- Teaching Textbook *
- Math Mammoth

Science

- Abeka
- Real Science Odyssey
- CrossWired Science (Multi-grade learning)
- Apologia *

* I have used these curriculums

HOMESCHOOL VOCABULARY

Accreditation – Verification that an institution meets quality standards.

ACT Test – Entrance exam required by colleges and universities. Includes a science section and tests higher-level math compared to the SAT exam.

AP Test – Advanced placement tests are given to high school students who want to earn college credits while still in high school.

Assessment – Some states require this evaluation to demonstrate a student's progress. Many homeschoolers use this test to develop and implement unique teaching strategies for future lessons.

Auditory learner – Student who absorbs information better by listening and speaking.

Bernoulli's equation – Velocity and static pressure of movement.

Charlotte Mason – Method that believes in educating the person as a whole and not just the mind by exposing children to living books, music, art, and poetry.

Common Core – Created in 2010 to bring the education system of all states into alignment. It is meant to create high-quality education.

Concept mapping – Graphical representation used to reorganize information and recognize the connection between concepts.

CO-OP – When homeschool families get together and each parent teaches a specific subject.

Correspondence school – Homeschoolers learn at home, but have guidance from the school.

Counselor – Guidance counselors provide assistance in choosing curriculum and preparing students for college.

Cover school – Also known as umbrella school.

CPALMS – Interactive tool to help implement teaching guidelines.

Diagnostic test – Identifies previous knowledge and detects areas that need reinforcement or intervention.

Diploma – Confirms a student has completed high school. Parent-generated diplomas are not always accepted by universities.

Distance learning – Classes are conducted online. Homeschoolers can choose to take a few online classes through accredited institutions.

Dual enrollment – Home-schoolers take college classes and earn credits while still in high school. Program is free for homeschoolers.

Duke TIP Talent Search – Duke University's talent identification program identifies students who are scholastically gifted.

Eclectic curriculum – Individualized education where parents combine different resources.

Electives – Classes that are outside the core curriculum.

Enrichment program – Includes activities outside the core curriculum that give students the opportunity to explore their interests.

EOC test – End of year tests required by public schools and available to homeschoolers who take online classes from state virtual schools.

FCAT – Florida assessment test given annually to public school students that is also available to homeschoolers.

Flashcards – Learning tool to learn facts. Pictures can be used for visual learners.

Formative assessment – Identifies gaps and assesses student's knowledge.

GED – Equivalent to a high school diploma, but not viewed as a good replacement by universities.

GPA – Grade point average is the average of a student's accumulated final grades.

Homeschool convention – A gathering of parents, students, vendors, and speakers.

Honor Society – An organization that recognizes high school students who excel academically.

HSLDA – Home School Legal Defense Association protects homeschoolers' rights.

IOWA Test – Nationally normed standardized test. This test compares students' abilities across the country, from private schools to homeschoolers.

Kinesthetic learning – Tactile learners absorb information through touching.
Knuckle Mnemonic – Memory aid for remembering how many days each month has.

Learning styles – The most popular modalities are kinesthetic, auditory, and visual learning.
Letter of intent – A letter used to notify the department of education of your intention to homeschool.

Mastery approach – The mastery approach requires complete understanding of a concept before moving on to a new topic.
Mnemonics – Mnemonics are simple strategies that can be used to aid information retention.

No Child Left Behind Act – Created to set high standards and measurable goals to improve education.

Parenting styles – Authoritarian, permissive, authoritative, and uninvolved.
Piaget theory – Defines the four stages of children's cognitive development.
PIAT – The Peabody Individual Achievement Test is administered by a trained examiner. Homeschoolers can choose oral or written test.
PISA – Program for International Student Assessment tests high school students around the world.
Placement test – Tests a student's academic skills to determine appropriate courses or classes.
Portfolio – A portfolio documents student's educational choices and progress.

SACs accreditation – Southern Association of Colleges and Schools is one of six regional accreditation organizations that monitors and evaluates schools.
SAT – Universities require students to take the SAT or ACT exam to be admitted into an undergraduate program.

Shadowing – Job shadowing offers hands-on experience to explore different fields.

Spiral approach – The spiral method introduces a topic and moves on to a new theme, even if students did not master the concept.

Star system – A calendar system where children earn a sticker when making the right choices. Stars can be exchanged for extra video game time or anything listed on the child's fun activity list.

Summative assessment – Graded tests administered by teachers at the end of each lesson.

Sunshine Standards – Now known as Generation Sunshine State Standards (NGSSS) defines what students need to learn from first through 12th grade.

Supplementing – Augmenting student's education or providing remedial work.

Support group – Provides opportunities for socialization, monthly meetings, yearbook, co-ops, proms, science fairs, and standardized tests.

Trade school – Trade schools teach skills related to jobs, such as welding or plumbing. This is a great option for a reluctant learner who wants to get into the job market faster.

Traditional school – Teacher-centered education, where instruction is delivered to a group of students in a school setting.

Transcript – Lays out student's courses, grades, and GPA. It is used to determine eligibility for university admission.

Umbrella school (cover school) – The definition varies from school to school. Some may offer standardized tests, defined curriculum, and field trips. Others may just offer support, and the student is still considered a homeschooler.

VAK – Visual, auditory, and kinesthetic learning strategies.

Virtual school – Online instruction offered by private and public schools.

Visual learner – One of the three learning styles. Visual learners prefer pictures, maps, educational shows, and any other visual media.

ABOUT THE AUTHOR

Eloisa Minasi is an electrical engineer, teacher, and writer. She is an adviser for homeschool support groups and college students in Brazil and United States.

Currently, she is an engineering consultant. She volunteered as a scout leader, technical consultant for the FTC robot competition, and taught religious education for special needs children. Her Blog "Homeschooling for Academic Success – From Homeschool to Harvard without Paying a Cent." has helped thousands of homeschooler in North and South America.

INDEX

A

Accredited school 142, 145, 146, 152, 155, 157, 159, 163
Accuplacer, Pert, or Compass Tests 163
American History 56, 75, 79, 81, 82, 123, 124, 129, 145, 153, 158, 192
Animation series by Preston Blair 134
Annual assessment 51, 68, 78, 182
Annual evaluation 51, 53, 55, 72
Art 20, 23, 58, 60, 80, 81, 82, 84, 107, 132, 134, 141, 142, 215
Articulation screen tests 25
Auditory learner 215

B

Barron's SAT Writing Workbook 105
BrainPOP 116
Butterfly garden kit 118

C

Civics 75, 129
Civil War 66, 123, 124
CLEP EXAM 159
Constructive feedback 184
Co-op 36, 56, 144, 146, 148, 149, 150
Critical-thinking skills 33, 118, 123, 130, 180
Curriculum 1, 4, 5, 9, 13, 14, 16, 18, 20, 21, 24, 28, 36, 44, 45, 46, 47, 51, 54, 55, 56, 59, 66, 68, 69, 71, 77, 78, 80, 81, 82, 83, 85, 86, 87, 88, 89, 91, 97, 98, 99, 101, 105, 111, 115, 116, 117, 118, 123, 124, 126, 129, 136, 137, 139, 141, 143, 147, 148, 149, 150, 151, 152, 154, 155, 157, 159, 210, 211, 212, 215, 216, 218
Cursive writing 106

D

Dealing with anger 179
Dealing with bad behavior 167
Discipline 11, 15, 31, 169, 179, 181, 183, 184, 185, 191
Drawing: Landscapes with William Powell 134
Dual enrollment 153, 160, 216
Duke TIP Talent Search 216
Dweck, Carol S. Ph. D. 46, 90, 94, 207

E

English 10, 16, 23, 28, 29, 54, 79, 80, 81, 82, 84, 104, 106, 111, 113, 141, 146, 150, 155, 158, 166, 183, 197
EOC test 75, 216
Exploration Education 117
Exploring Creation With General Science 116
Exploring Creation With Physical Science 116
Extrovert 73, 194

F

Field trips 4, 34, 38, 53, 59, 60, 62, 64, 66, 115, 116, 133, 148, 149, 150, 200, 218
   Virtual 66
Financial expenditure 56
Flexibility 4, 18, 55, 153, 180, 193
Florida Virtual School 36, 75, 146
Foreign language 28, 29, 58, 81, 82, 141, 174, 190
Formative assessments 69

G

Geography 20, 23, 29, 42, 58, 61, 79, 82, 84, 122, 123, 124, 126, 128, 129, 136, 150
Gettysburg DVD 123

H

Harvard 1, 3, 11, 24, 81, 133, 140, 201, 202, 208, 210
Hatchery frog kit 118
Highlights Top Secret 128
High school class requirementS 80
History 5, 16, 20, 22, 42, 58, 61, 66, 70, 79, 81, 84, 109, 116, 122, 123, 124, 125, 126, 128, 129, 134, 136, 141, 142, 145, 149, 156, 186, 192
Homeschoolers' experiences at Harvard 201
Homeschooling law 77, 157
How to handle failure 41

I

Illustory Make-A-Book 106
Institute for Excellence in Writing 99
Introvert 73, 194
Iowa Test of Basic Skills 71
Iowa Test Practice Book 71

K

Kinesthetic learner 64, 77, 78

L

Learning how to read 108
Learning Language Arts Through Literature 111
Learn to Write the Novel Way 105

M

Map Tangle 127
Mastery approach 217
Math Drill Express 87
Mavis Beacon Teaches Typing 134
Mindstorms 173
Mnemonics 20, 26, 217
Music 20, 23, 58, 59, 79, 80, 81, 82, 84, 105, 120, 132, 133, 134, 141, 142, 149, 166, 173, 208, 215
My Name Is America 109, 124

N

National Wildlife Federation 118
Negative feedback 184, 185
Never give up 197
Notice of intent 52

O

Online classes 75, 80, 146, 162, 205, 216

P

Parenting style 179
Part-time homeschooling 4, 14, 15
Peabody Individual Achievement Test 72, 73, 217
Peer pressure 4, 170, 172, 197
Phonics reading 109
Piaget's theory 113, 191
PIAT test 72, 217
Portfolio 44, 52, 53, 84, 217
Positive relationship 178
Public-school standards 84
Public speaking 35

Q

Quizlet 42, 102, 111, 130

R

Reader's Edge 112
Reading 10, 24, 33, 42, 46, 53, 56, 64, 68, 69, 71, 72, 73, 74, 79, 86, 109, 110, 111, 112, 123, 126, 140, 163, 193
Reading comprehension 71, 72, 73, 112, 163
Rosetta Stone 28
Rules 26, 30, 35, 50, 88, 92, 97, 98, 99, 149, 152, 159, 160, 161, 163, 167, 169, 170, 171, 175, 176, 178, 179, 180, 185, 186, 197

S

SAT 12, 74, 75, 105, 150, 152, 153, 154, 156, 159, 160, 161, 162, 163, 188, 215, 217
  Adversity score 163
  Subject tests 152, 153, 156, 163
Saxon 18, 21, 41
  Placement tests 41
Schedule 5, 16, 18, 56, 58, 59, 75, 83, 115, 204
School system flaws 10, 13, 46, 97, 177
Science 4, 10, 11, 13, 15, 16, 18, 33, 36, 58, 61, 64, 66, 68, 70, 71, 72, 73, 74, 79, 80, 81, 82, 84, 106, 115, 116, 117, 118, 119, 120, 138, 141, 142, 143, 150, 155, 156, 164, 174, 192, 205, 215, 218
  Experiments 70, 119
  National Honor Society 188
Scoring High Iowa Tests 72, 74
Sensory play 119
Seton Home Study School 146, 152
Sibling fighting 175
SimCity™ software 129
Socialization 4, 34, 35, 44, 205, 218
SparkNotes 110
Speech 25, 26, 111, 190, 209
Standardized test 37, 47, 52, 54, 68, 70, 72, 73, 74, 75, 147, 148, 217
STARS® 112
State History 125
State Standards 82, 83, 218
Stop whining 175
Story of the World 123, 212
Strictest states to homeschool 53
Supplementing 1, 4, 14, 218
Support groups 44, 50, 150

T

Teacher's ID 150
Teaching Textbook 88, 212
Teenage years 168, 169
Test-taking benefits 74
Theater 132, 142
Time Travelers 123
Traditional homeschoolers 152, 153
Transitioning from a brick-and-mortar school to homeschool 18
Types of assessments 69

U

Umbrella school 80, 144, 146, 147, 148, 153, 215

V

Video Text Interactive 21, 88, 89, 92
Visual learner 24
Volunteering 17, 52, 137, 138, 139, 140, 161, 187, 205

W

Writing 5, 11, 14, 15, 33, 36, 51, 58, 68, 79, 92, 96, 97, 98, 99, 100, 101, 102, 104, 105, 106, 107, 109, 110, 111, 123, 126, 130, 137, 141, 142, 164
Writing Strands 98

Z

Zac the Rat from Starfall Education 109